"Are You Being Served?"

A Nostalgic "Down Memory Lane" reminder of some of the shops and business's that flourished in the Gosport of Yesteryear.

© RON BROWN

ISBN 0 903852 16 0

Printed by The Southern Press, Horndean, Hants.

Down Memory Lane

Published by
Milestone Publications
62 Murray Road
Horndean
Hants PO8 9JL

D1798681

Sponsored by
HOMELINE
The Nationwide Home Selling Service.
"The real alternative to estate agents. And their fees"

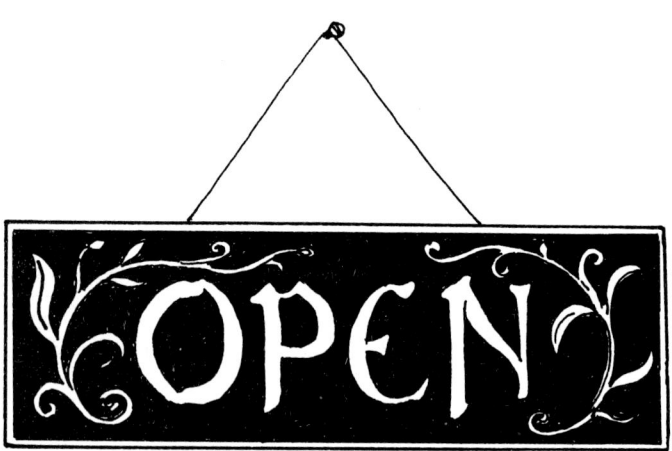

Young Tommy sat playing with his toys in the family living room, they only had one bedroom in the humble little dwelling that they rented, and that he had to share with his mum and dad. His father had been working on the night shift at the brewery nearby all night, and at this very moment was snoring away to his hearts content in the room above, hence Tommy being confined to the living room.

His collection of toys did not really amount to much, but at that moment he had on the rug in front of him his treasured collection of lead soldiers that good old Uncle Fred had given him on his last birthday. An event that nicely coincided with the fact that Uncle Fred had enjoyed a good win on the dogs!

Like most lads, Tommy had broken off the heads of the toy soldiers, then joined the parts together with a matchstick, thus allowing the head to move in all directions, a very useful ploy when lead troops are being attacked from behind! He was just planning his battle campaign, when a voice shrilled through from the scullery. "Tommy, come here a minute".

It was his mother, and as the boy went through to where she was, she was engrossed in counting out coins from her tattered purse onto a shopping list on the table before her. "Just pop up to Watt's corner shop with this note, and fetch these few things back for me Tommy". And as he reached the door, she called "Mind you don't lose the money".

Tommy did not mind going into Mr. Watt's grocery shop, it at least provided an excuse to get nearer to those glass jars full of multi-coloured sweets that have such an hypnotic effect on children of all ages. Another attraction was the aroma of the shop, absolutely unique. How can you possibly describe that smell, a mixture of bacon, tea, coffee, ham, tarry firelighters and paraffin, with overtones of apples, sprouts and spring onions!

Mr. Watt's bushy white eyebrows appeared to raise at least two inches as the boy approached the counter, and his large red cheeks appeared to take on an even darker hue. "And what can I do for you young fellow"? Whereupon Tommy placed the by now crumpled piece of paper on top of the counter, the grocer gave an understanding nod and went about his business.

Mr. Watt went methodically through the list, there appeared to be nothing that he could not produce from the shelves of his veritable 'Aladdins Cave' of a provision store. With the dexterity of a conjuror, by wielding his wooden pat he would produce from a large portion of butter a neat little package that was as squarely proportioned as if it had been produced by a machine.

Also without the aid of any mechanical adding devices, he had the bill added-up in a trice. But even then, he had not failed to notice little Tommy staring at the sweet jars whilst the operation had taken place. "There we are my lad, all ready, and give your mother my regards". Then, with a twinkle in his eye as the boy gathered up his mum's wicker basket, "Oh, you might as well help yourself to a sherbet dab on the way out".

Of course, Tommy did not need any second telling, and once out of the store he skipped merrily down the street to the door of his house that faced straight onto the pavement. First taking the groceries through to mum, then settling down to the serious business of devouring a sherbet dab! No, Tommy certainly had no objection to doing any shopping for his mum, if it should end in rewards such as sweets, and of course it usually did!

I would suspect that the above little 'slice of life' tale will bring back to many readers memories of their youth, in which they also were sent down to the corner shop at what appeared to be very regular intervals. In the old days, folk did not seem to buy large amounts of goods all in one go, they appeared to wait until they had almost run out of the commodity that they required. Hence Mrs. Jones from next door always calling over the back garden fence to borrow a cup of sugar!

Of course, it is the shops that have really changed so much over the years, it is becoming increasingly difficult to find the friendly little corner shop, they are being replaced by glass-plated aluminiumised goldfish bowls with uninteresting exteriors, languishing in concrete shopping precincts like cardboard boxes on a shelf.

The windows of modern shops all appear to be the same, generally plastered with masses of paper and cardboard guff proclaiming that they have 10p off the price of soap powder, or that you get ten per cent more cornflakes in a packet for the same price!

Certainly they had plenty of advertisements in the old days, but somehow they appeared to be in better taste and quality. They took a pride in the art work, in fact many of the old signs of yesteryear have become collectors items now. The metal signs that were proudly displayed on shop exteriors were exquisitely produced, 'Frys Cocoa', 'Lyons Cakes', 'Mazawattee Tea', 'Mumbys Table Waters', 'Cadburys Cocoa', 'Wellingtons Oakey Knife Polish', the list could seemingly go on and on.

The old traders had a strong faith in the power of advertising and to get the sales message across they employed any blank space that moved, or did not move. First the new-fangled street trams, and later the motor buses, were the objects of their advertising, even the vehicle 'Stop' posts were utilized along with the street lamp standards. Also crossing the harbour did not escape their attention, the now extinct floating bridges were plastered with masses of advertising posters, as were the hoardings surrounding the old Hard area.

If the shops have changed so much, then certainly the people that serve behind the counters have, that is if they have a counter still, for there is a great abundance of self service. It is becoming increasingly difficult to find the Mr. Watt's in our modern world, one has to queue to pass through a robot-type check-out, and as yet these machines cannot smile pleasantly or pass the time of day, or give free sweets to the youngsters!

And that of course is the whole crunch of the matter, machines are catering for the rush and tear-about days that we now live in, with the lady of the house very often holding down a job as well, time is the essence. It was so much more leisurely in the old days, going to the little shop was an event, in which you not only obtained your daily requirements, but also learnt interesting snippets of information about what was going on in the local community. "Did you know Mrs. Murphy is expecting again"? "Is she, that must be her sixth"!

But one of the better factors about modern life is the working hours, before the last war it appeared that many of the shops never seemed to close, a definite case of 'open all hours'. All very nice for the shopkeeper, but pity the poor assistants, Sundays could not come around quick enough, and probably half of that day of rest they spent in going to church.

The long opening hours were brought about by the advent of gas lamps on our streets, before this most folk only went out shopping in daylight hours, they were frightened of being accosted by footpads and muggers So whilst street lighting was good news for shoppers and shopkeepers, it was bad news for shop assistants.

The town of Gosport, unlike so many of its neighbours, has not to any great extent attracted the attention of large departmental stores or organizations, or undergone great structural alterations to provide covered-in shopping precincts. It has always been a town of small shops, providing individual service to the customer. This may be pure conjecture on my part, but at the end of the day the small shops could be Gosport's great sales attraction, people could get disenchanted with rows of stores that all present the same glass plated image. Covered-in precincts may be fine in the wet weather, but they also blot out the sunshine and fresh air, giving shop workers the same conditions as living in a submarine.

Gosport's High Street has managed to retain much of its character, and Stoke Road even more so, the traders still strive to provide that personal touch, and it is rather amazing, one can very often get an item from these unique little shops that the larger department stores cannot be bothered to stock. As you may gather, what I am trying to say is, 'small can be beautiful'.

The whole object of this humble publication is to have a "Down Memory Lane" style reminder of some of the shops and businesses that flourished in the Gosport of Yesteryear. It not only relates to food provision establishments, but as you will see, a wide variety of trades and goods.

As you may imagine, it is a most formidable task, and I know that I cannot possibly hope to keep everyone happy by mentioning their particular favourite store, where they may have obtained their choicest joint of meat, or most stretchable yard of elastic. But never the less, I hope it will serve to provide some nostalgic memories of youth for older readers, and at the same time for the younger readers an idea of what life was like in earlier times, and in particular some of the towns traders who served our daily needs.

But before you reach for your purse and shopping bag, let me warn you that it is inevitable that I shall have to mention prices, and that they will be given in what we now term as 'old money'. In other words, pounds, shillings, and pence. Please do not be too alarmed, remember, the average wage in those days was also low to go along with the prices!

Right, now you can pick-up your shopping basket, don't forget to close the front door, and don't forget to take the key with you. What am I talking about? In those trusting far-off days we always had a spare key hanging on a piece of string behind the letter-box!

CHAPTER ONE

"Mum said, can you put it on the slate?"

One facility that the modern superstore cannot provide is in letting their customers settle-up their account on pay day, this was something the old shopkeeper was very pleased to do, he might lose trade otherwise. But of course, he knew his customers, he recognized them as poor but honest working folk, who were forced generally to live from day to day. Even if they had the money, it was not so easy to stock up on certain provisions, for they did not have the advantage that a modern refrigerator can provide.

Another factor in comparison between old and modern methods of shopping, is that self-service can miss out on what is known in the trade as 'the extra sale'. Our shopkeeper of old had this off to a fine art, whilst packing up his customers requisites, he would say: "There we are Madam, by the way, I see you have not got ham on your list, it so happens that out back I have just taken delivery of a joint, it is fresh, and I can slice you some off if you wish". This ploy is what selling is all about, when they sold a lamp shade: "Oh, are you all right for light bulbs Madam?" So you may see, the modern self-service take-it or leave-it methods are by no means perfect, neither for the shopper or the shopkeeper. It really all comes down to personal service.

I cannot hope to mention them all of course, but Gosport in days gone by certainly had its fair share of grocery stores. Back in the middle of the last century, there were over eighty grocery or provision stores trading in the area, including Elson, Forton and Alverstoke.

Although this goes back beyond living memory, there was a name from those days that will be familiar with townsfolk, the name of Thorngate. This business was run by three hard working brothers, who lived only for their store, and so remained bachelors. The building was sited on the corner of Southcross and High Street, an old fashioned, but rather imposing building for those times in a small town such as Gosport. The shop windows comprised many small panes of glass, and they were lit at night by dozens of candles. Digressing for a moment, it may be interesting to note that plate glass windows were first introduced in Gosport in 1845, but not by the Thorngate's.

Although they were primarily grocers and provision merchants, the Thorngate brothers were not adverse to selling anything that would bring in money, and the store was more like a bazaar, a sort of early Woolworth's.

The Thorngate boys were not great ones for throwing their money around, they could show a very mean streak. When Mr. Laming the water carrier came around with his water barrel cart, rather than pay him one farthing a bucket for it, they preferred to walk down to the public pump farther down the High Street to carry out their daily ablutions. A rather chilly practice in the winter!

But I am pleased to say, rather like our old Dickens friend, Scrooge, they came good in the end, and their generosity still abounds to this day. In 1865 Thorngate money was responsible for providing 64 almshouses in the Brockhurst and Forton areas, folk living in them were paid 10/- every Friday, coal was provided, and sometimes a few little extras. There was also the Thorngate Free Dispensary in the High Street, a home for female servants when out of work, a wash house in South Street, and of course the first Thorngate Halls that were built in 1885 at a cost of £9,000 as a memorial to William Thorngate. Yes, I think it would be fair to say that the Thorngate family certainly left their mark on the town.

John Thorngate was at one time a member of the Town Trustees, and was perhaps one of the first in a long line of Gosport shopkeepers to play a part in the running of the towns affairs. I know that many will make the usual comment about local business people serving on councils and governing bodies, only there to line their own pockets, and generally subject them with titles, such as 'The Forty Thieves'. But this is a little unfair, for many of the early business men did a great deal to build Gosport from a small fishing village to the civic status it enjoys today.

The Thorngate business site at 132, High Street, was later taken over by another famous Gosport establishment, Messrs. Hoare & Pilcher, and for many years it has been occupied by the Portsea Island Mutual Co-operative Society grocery branch. But I am jumping the gun a little, let us go back to the 1950's.

Further along the High Street at number 111, Mr. Arthur Wright was proprietor of a very prosperous grocery store, but it is the gentleman who took the business over from Arthur that will be better remembered, Mr. George Cooke. George came to Gosport in 1871, and from No. 111 he built up one of the largest provision establishments in the town, and indeed in Portsmouth, for he used to wholesale goods to shops across the water.

Born in Hereford, George Cooke had the grocery business in his blood, for his father was also a grocer in those parts. George certainly had his head screwed on the right way, for as well as being an astute business man, in 1874 he married the only daughter of Colonel Charles Mumby, the Mineral Water King.

But apart from the usual food lines, George did rather well selling something a bit stronger than mineral waters, and conducted a flourishing wine, spirit and beer trade. Of course, this was in the days when you could buy a bottle of good whisky such as Gilbey's 'Glen Spey' for only four shillings, or a bottle of Fine Jamaica Rum for 2/8d. a bottle! You could hardly get a couple of packets of crisps for that now!

The name of Cooke spread far and wide, he made sure it did, being a great believer in the power of advertising, ferry passengers alighting from the ferry could hardly miss the name, it was in letters four feet high!

But with an army of workers keeping his business turning over nicely, George Cooke devoted a great deal of his fantastic energy to the towns affairs. He was on the Council for the Urban District of Gosport for 25 years, he was invited to become its first Chairman, but stood down in favour of Dr. Kealy, although he did in actual fact become Chairman himself a few years later. Being something of a financial wizard, his presence benefitted the town greatly, but his pet object appeared to be with education. His dream was for the establishment of a Secondary School in the town, and almost entirely due to his efforts this became a reality in 1902, the school being built in the old library complex, now the Gosport Museum.

A great character of the town, George was a familiar sight riding around on his old bicycle, a practice he relinquished after nearly being killed by a car coming from behind a tram. George Cooke did in fact pass on to the 'Great Grocer in the Sky' in 1918 at the age of 71, only three weeks after he had learnt that his only son had been killed in France.

Another grocer took over Cooke's premises at No. 111, which by now had been expanded to No. 112 as well, this was Reginald Smith. But in later years by the 1930's it was run by Gorman's Stores, who also had another shop in Stoke Road at No. 49. Smith had also previously owned the Stoke Road premises, this was taken over by J. P. Gray going under the banner of the 'Richmond Stores', then Gorman took it over from him.

Gorman sold out the shop at 111, High Street next to the old Post Office, and Burton's Menswear shop has operated from the site since the late 30's. Gorman continued for a number of years at his Stoke Road branch, although he nearly lost it through fire in 1928. One Sunday morning of that year P. C. Jackson was on his beat down Stoke Road, when he noticed that No. 49 was filled with smoke, and that the window blind was smouldering. Acting quickly, he broke into the rear of the premises and tore down the blinds to pull them out back. Evidently the fire had been caused through the suns rays shining through a small crack in the plate glass windows.

Not far away from Gorman's in Stoke Road, down at No.19 & 20 was the premises of Messrs. Wilson & Son on the corner of Joseph Street. This was one of the old established family grocers, who were in business from the same site for over 50 years. John Wilson took the business over from his father, until he himself died in 1923 at the age of 67. As well as food and bread, Wilson's were also wine and spirit merchants. That in fact is the trade for which this particular corner site will be most remembered, for it was taken over in later years by Smeed & Smeed, and within recent years it has become 'Carousel', a ladies and childrens outfitters.

When I mentioned earlier that many of the old grocers seemed to stocked everything under the sun, this has highlighted the difficulty in trying to split the various trades, for many grocers also stocked bread, often baked on the premises, and even sold meat. Skinner Brothers were a fine example of this, sited in Brockhurst on the corner of Avery Lane, although they were noted for their bread, they also were not adverse to selling anything else that was consumable.

Another family establishment that was renowned for their bread was Rogers in North Street, although officially they were listed as grocers. Richard Rogers originated in the Isle of Wight, he came to Gosport in the last century to start a bakery

Skinner Brothers Grocers Shop,
corner of Avery Lane.

and provision shop at No. 86 North Street, he had two sons, Fred and Sanders, who also worked in the family business. Fred also got very involved with Gosport's public life, serving on the Alverstoke Board of Guardians, whilst Sanders favoured the more social happenings in the town, being one of the prime instigators behind the famous Grove Pageants, writing and producing most of the shows held in the early years of this century. it is inevitable that the Roger's name will crop up again in my section on the towns bakers.

Many older residents of the town will have fond memories of Mrs. Cooper's little grocery shop, also in North Street.One day, this lady nearly lost her shop, and nearly half of North Street with it! Gas fitter Henry Pavey of Kings Road was attending to a gas pipe in her shop, he had the cap off to grease a thread, when his rather inquisitive mate who was holding a candle for illumination got a little too close! Whooomph! Luckily, on this occasion it was only a case of waving goodbye to Henry's eyebrows! We often hear of prices going up, but very seldom of shops going the same way!

Oh, those marvellous household names of days gone by, establishments that appear to have disappeared from our main streets. Let me give you a short reminder with the following: Maypole Dairies, Lipton's, and Colonial, the International Tea Company, the World's Stores, alas, famous names we can no longer boast in Gosport.

Of course, these establishments formed part of a country-wide chain of provision stores. There is another well known name that I did not include in the above, that of W. Pink and Sons. They also had a vast chain of stores, but originating in Portsmouth, this family business has strong local associations. It is also one of the last remaining grocers that I can remember of what I fondly term the old style, marvellous smells would hit you as you walked into the Gosport branch in the High Street, oh! if only that delicious and unique aroma could have been captured and bottled.

It all began with one man, William Pink, he was born at Greenwood Farm near Bishops Waltham. A member of the well known Pink family of Winchester, one of his ancestors was the Mayor of Winchester back in 1689. When a mere lad, William served as an apprentice in a Winchester grocers, but as soon as he was able he went off to London to seek his fortune. He returned to Hampshire a few years later to take up a position as manager of Earl's Grocery Store at 112, Commercial Road in Portsmouth.

Eager to get on, he returned once again to London, and eventually joined Fortnum & Mason of Piccadilly, grocers to

*George Cooke's in the High Street, c. 1905.
Now Burton's Menswear.*

the gentry. He did well, managed to save some money, and at the ripe old age of 28 he returned to Portsmouth to buy the business of his former employers, Earl's in Commercial Road.

The year was 1858, and Commercial Road in those days was not exactly the bustling shopping area we know today, what is more, William Pink's store was not exactly on a prime site, sandwiched between a stonemasons yard on one side, and a secondhand store on the other. But with William's vitality for hard work, sometimes working seventeen hours a day, the shop succeeded. He took over the stonemasons yard, and also the premises on his other side, which by then was Smith's Eating House, and the whole site became known as Pink's Corner.

Carnival Parade outside Pink's in the High Street.

But I am afraid this vast grocery empire began to dwindle after the last war, and the branches can now be counted on one hand. The Gosport High Street branch closed in the 1960s, but it is worth mentioning that at one time they had two other Pink's branches in the town, one was in St. Thomas's Road at Hardway, the other in Brockhurst Road on the corner of Harding Road.

Also, we must not forget the dear old Co-op, for back in the 1930's the Portsea Island Mutual Co-operative Society had at least five grocery stores in the Gosport area. Slowly, they appear to be closing shops throughout the Portsmouth area, although the High Street grocery department of the Co-op is still surviving on the corner of South Cross Street, in fact where Thorngates had their store so many years ago.

There is one more well known grocer from the past that I have to mention, in fact from small beginnings he also succeeded in the wholesale supply of provisions in a big way, his name was John Parham. John first came to Gosport in 1860 to start a small grocery business in the Camden area of Forton, with the help of only one assistant.

His son Leonard was born over that shop in 1863, and he was destined to play a big role in the growth of Gosport in later years, but his life was nearly cut off before it had hardly started. When Leonard was one month old, the Forton Road corner shop caught fire, his father out at a watch night service in the Wesleyan Church, had left his baby on at home with his wife, it was New Years Eve. As he was nearing home on his return journey, John Parham found the premises were ablaze. He raised the alarm, and after a desperate struggle, the mother and child were thankfully saved.

John Parham built his grocery business to such an extent, he was eventually able to open a large store in Forton Road primarily for wholesale supplies. John was very much involved

In 1887 the shop facia was changed to 'W. Pink & Sons', he took into partnership his three sons, Ernest, Harold, and Victor. The family lived on the Commercial Road premises, in fact, Sir Harold Pink, as he became later, was actually born in the room that in later years was to become his office. Of course, Harold served as Mayor of Portsmouth several terms.

The founder, William Pink, died in 1906, leaving his sons to carry on the business, and this they did with gusto, the name of the game was expansion, branches began to sprout all over the area. In 1914, Pink's had 12 shops and employed 314 staff, and by 1920 they had 25 shops with 507 staff. Owing to the rapid growth of the firm, in 1933 it became a limited company, by then they had 44 branches employing 700 people.

Gray's in Stoke Road, 1912.
Later taken over by Gorman's.

with the towns affairs, serving as a member of the Local Board. For the services he rendered, like many other of Gosport's notables, he had a street named after him, hence Parham Road. His store was on one corner, and he also owned the land from the opposite corner to Ferroll Road, upon which was sited his family residence known as Forton Lodge.

The name of Parham was on every Gosport residents lips in 1907, for in that year a big robbery ring was uncovered at the store. Seven men, all employed at Parham's, were charged with burglary, it involved the theft of tea, butter, and other foods. Following this, three Gosport traders appeared in court charged with receiving stolen goods, mostly concerning tobacco. The three were Charles Fish, landlord of the 'Fox' public house in North Street, a hairdresser named John Confer, and Albert Lee, an outfitters manager.

Anyway, even allowing for pilferers, the business of Parham & Son continued to flourish, and by 1913 they were employing a staff of 40 in Forton Road, and were able to enjoy an annual turnover of £100,000. Which, I think you will agree, was an awful lot of lolly in 1913!

John Parham died in 1918, sadly missed by the town, and more especially by the members of the Weslyan Church, for he had assisted financially to a great extent in the building of their new church in Stoke Road. His son Leonard carried on the business, and he also did good work on the Urban District Council, being elected Chairman in 1908.

That site on the corner of Parham Road will be remembered in later years as the premises for Ivens, Kelletts & Childs, also wholesale grocers. In more recent years, the premises have been taken over by timber merchants W. H. Wheeler & Sons, who in fact had their works adjacent to I.K.C. dating back before the Second World War.

As I stated at the beginning, the list of Gosport's grocers through the years could almost fill a telephone directory on its own, but I hope I have touched upon enough names from the past to start your nostalgic taste buds watering. In 1969 in Gosport, there were 115 grocers, and eight supermarkets. It is a different story now, twelve years later, current figures show that 60p. in every £1 goes into the tills of supermarkets, and small grocers are disappearing from our streets at a steady rate. In fact, the number of food shops in the High Street can be numbered on one hand, in this once bustling throughfare that could once boast so many big national names.

It has become increasingly difficult for the small grocer, resulting in tradesmen such as Harry Cook having to close his Village Stores in Alverstoke in February 1981, after 35 years trading. It was significant that many regular customers, including local children, went into the shop to bid Harry a sad farewell. This highlights what I have stated previously about personal service.

Before we leave grocers to look at other tradesfolk of the past, let me give you a reminder of some of the old prices that we paid for our essentials. In 1901 you had to pay 2d. for a pound of sugar, in a blue bag of course, and by 1920 this had leapt to 6d. a pound! One dozen eggs in 1900 would have cost you 1/2d., and a pound of butter would also have set you back 1/2d. The Chancellor of the Exchequer in our house tells me that she is currently paying 83p. for a pound of butter, and this of course is around 16/6d. in old money. When you look at these figures, they are not so alarming as they may seem when compared with the average wage nowadays. Having said that, I will probably get every old age pensioner in Hampshire trying to hit me with their umbrellas! But let us go on to another food product.

CHAPTER TWO

"Give Unto Us Our Daily Bread"

For pure nostalgia, I must admit that my favourite adverts on television are the ones for Hovis Bread, especially where the little lad in the cloth cap tramps over the bleak cobbled streets, fiercely clutching a loaf to his coat. He gets home, takes off his cap, and triumphantly lays the bread on the kitchen table to receive a beaming smile from his Mum. Ah, the memories come flooding back!

This serves as a reminder that bread for many of us, was indeed the staff of life. Running home from school, eager to sink our little molars into hunks of crusty bread, spread with butter if we were lucky, and maybe lashings of home-made jam! All washed down with a mug of tea that you could almost stand your spoon up in! Lovely Stuff!

Of course, as youngsters we were so busy scoffing the stuff, that not much thought was given as to how the bread was made, it just magically appeared onto our tables via the bakers shop on the corner. In fact being a baker, is not everyones cup of tea, or perhaps I should say, piece of cake. It calls for long hours in sometimes unpleasant conditions of heat, commenced at a time of day when most folk are still in the land of nod. The trademark of most bakers, is their pasty faces!

Let me now have a reminder of some of the best known pasty faces of Gosport in earlier days, there were certainly plenty of them. Back in the 1850's there appears to have been approximately twenty official bakers in operation, none of the names will really strike a bell now, but it is interesting to note that at least two of them remained the sites for subsequent bakeries. In 1859 Henry Robinson ran his bakers shop from No. 6 North Street, in later years this was taken over for the

Gosport High Street, 1920's.

same purpose by Fred Fry, older readers will remember his shop on the corner of Sea Horse Street.

Further down the road, at No. 86 North Street, there was the bakery of William Paul, this was later to become the establishment of the previously mentioned Rogers family of bakers and grocers. By the 1930's these same premises in North Street had been taken over by Messrs. Smith & Vosper, Ltd, they also had branches in the High Street, and in Stoke Road.

The Stoke Road branch on the corner of Stone Lane had also previously been a bakers business, that of Frank Cooper. Frank was a Gosport chap, born at No. 3 Railway view in Albert Street in the year 1876. An energetic and enterprising man, he owned his own bakery business by 1900, this was formerly on the other corner of Stone Lane, the site now occupied by Barnes and Elliott the builders. Frank had a good helper in his wife Alice, whom he had married in 1896.

In 1906 the Cooper's moved across the road to the opposite corner of Stone Lane, in fact a stone was laid by Alice in the wall to commemorate the event, and is still there to this day. After baking the bread, Frank would have to go out and deliver it, this was generally to the more affluent areas of Alverstoke, such as the Crescent. But I am afraid Frank Cooper paid the price for his hard work, and died at the age of 34 in 1910. His wife Alice struggled on with the shop for some years after this on her own, but had to give it up in the end, and she died herself at the relatively young age of 54. That corner site has changed hands many times in the following years, and at the present moment it serves as the picture framing and art supplies shop of Tony and Pat Wing, known as the Stoke Gallery.

It is interesting to recall that during the latter half of the last century, many families had their Sunday dinners cooked in bakers shops. In fact, the bakers advertised in their windows: 'Housekeepers bread and dinners baked daily'. Small children would take a batch of dough which their mothers had made along to the shop, carefully wrapped in a clean white pillow slip. A favourite baker for this service was Frank Gray in Forton Road, and woe betide him if he failed to produce 25% on the weight of the flour used, or half the ladies in the neighbourhood would turn up the next day on his doorstep to tell him how it should be done.

I have fond memories of a grand old lady named Beatrice Watson, who lived to celebrate her 100th birthday. Beatrice was born in Tamworth Place off Alver road, and she told me how her family would drop off their Sunday dinner at the bakers whilst on the way to church, then pick it up cooked and ready for eating on the journey home, after paying a few coppers to the baker, of course!

But back to Stoke Road, on the corner of Shaftesbury Road stood another well known bakers, hands up those who remember Herbert Pyle. Herbert was a son of a Denmead farmer, and after school he served in a grocers store in Portsmouth for five years. He came to Fareham in 1883, first as a partner to his Uncle Mr. W. Pyle who had a confectioners establishment. Then Herbert branched out and purchased the Paragon Hotel in West Street next to Church Path, he converted it into a bakery, and named it the Paragon Bakery. He did well and expanded to open the Gosport branch in Stoke Road, still finding the time to serve as Chairman on the Fareham Urban District Council. A bakery still flourishes on the corner of Shaftesbury Road, this being Messrs. Wilkins.

A little farther down Stoke Road, most folk know of the bakers shop of Ursell's, this is in fact a very old name in the history of Gosport bakeries, their first shop being in Church Road Alverstoke, in the shadows of St. Mary's.

*Fred Carter going the rounds for
Marsh's Bakery.*

Walking from Stoke Road down Queens Road, on the corner of Sydney Road, in the early part of this century we would have seen Walt Harris selling bread from his bakers shop. I believe this site was taken over in later years by another well known baker of the town, our old friends Eager's Bakery. Many people will remember their shop down in the High Street, not far from the Swiss Restaurant. I recall John Eager, who now runs the Photo Shop in Stoke Road, telling me how as a lad he used to deliver trays of delicious cakes to the old 'Dive' cafe at the ferry, no doubt to be readily consumed by hungry tram and bus crews.

Mentioning Meotti's Swiss Cafe a few lines ago, I am sure brought memories flooding back to many readers, and strange-ly enough, this establishment was to feature in later years in connection with the bakery business. But before I explain that one, we shall have a reminder of another Gosport bakery from the past, the one popularly known as Marsh's.

Marsh and Son, operated from No. 78 Forton Road, and they certainly developed a large bread trade in the town. Although fairly wealthy, the boss Alfred Marsh was not exactly renowned for his generosity towards his employees. But he was a shrewd business man, and also a devout member of the Plymouth Brethren.

Fred Carter remembered those days well, he joined Marsh's Bakery at the age of 14, his uncle Mr. Birdwood Hedger was a foreman in the bakehouse there. Fred started work at eight shillings a week, on the understanding that when he could mould the bread he would get ten shillings a week. This was easier said than done, and it took poor Fred many months before he was proficient at it.

When he was 16 he was given one of the six delivery rounds, and off he would trot on his van, pulled by his faithful old horse "Topsy". Other delivery chaps at that time were Reg Adams, Charlie Ridgers and Harold Payne.

Marsh's went from strength to strength, one of the highlights being when they won the contract to supply bread for the Marines in Forton Barracks. When Fred drove the first load of bread through the barrack gates, he was treated like Royalty by a large crowd of cheering Marines. He worked for the Marsh family for over 38 years, and three other workers came from one family, the Allen's comprising brothers Leslie, Percy, and Harry.

They baked from 3.30 in the afternoon, until one o'clock in the morning. On Fridays, they worked all night, this was in preparation for the big demand for bread on the Saturday. Working in temperatures that would sap most people, the

"When bread was bread".
Frank Cooper's Bakery, Stoke Road.

bakers would help the long night pass quicker by having rousing singsongs, delving into hymns by the end of the shift. Harry Allen also remembers those days well, it would be true to say that the Allen family had bakery in their blood, and at one time had their own business in Inverness Road.

But back to Marsh's, difficult times were experienced during the last war, at times there was loss of electricity supply, and the mixing had to be done by hand. Cyril Marsh got over this by devising a petrol engine to operate the dough machine, a good example of the wartime spirit.

Alfred Marsh died, and son Cyril took over the business. But a year later, whilst out walking his dog, Cyril dropped dead, and that was the end of this popular bakery, the delivery vans of 'Marsh's Bakery' were never to rumble on the Gosport streets again.

Not very far away from Marsh's in Forton Road was another bakers in the form of the Tickner Brothers, they were sited on the corner of Mill Lane. Tickner's were really grocers as well as bakers, rather like those other brothers, the Skinner's, on the corner of Avery Lane and Brockhurst Road.

Before we leave bakery, we must finally look back on the history of another Gosport baker who indeed from very small beginnings, built what could only be described as a bakery empire. Most townsfolk over the age of forty, will remember Ayling's famous Hardway bakery.

The whole thing was started off by James Henry Ayling, who was born in 1859 in Gosport, coming from a long line of blacksmiths at Brockhurst. But hammers and anvils were not on the agenda for young James, he preferred a life on the ocean blue and so joined the Navy. Unfortunately, while still a young chap, he had to be invalided out, and found himself back in civvy street complete with a limp to remind him of his seagoing days.

But he found work in the little village store run by a Miss Pink, this was in St. Thomas's Road at Hardway. That shop just about sold everything, including bread. In the 1880's Miss Pink retired, and James bought the business from her for around £40, this included the horse and delivery cart!

The Ayling empire bagan to expand rapidly, with James investing in property around the Hardway area. He particularly concentrated on the bread trade, and opened a bakehouse in nearby Chapel Street. These were the days when faggot ovens were used for baking bread, and what lovely tasty loaves they were.

James Ayling met Miss Sophie Drover, their hearts went 'Boing', and before long they were tripping up the aisle. This union produced two daughters, May and Elsie, and one son named William. William later entered his fathers business, so he was ready to take over the helm when James Henry died in 1916 at the age of 56.

Under William, the business expanded even more, with new plant machinery and in general a more modern approach to the trade. The lovable old horses who clip-clopped around the streets of Gosport pulling their vans, were eventually replaced by motor vans. In fact, Ayling's always kept up to date with their delivery vehicles, and when the sale of buns and cakes became popular on the street rounds, they were one of the first bakers to have special compartments incorporated in their vans to hold the tasty additions. They were also one of the first bakers to use electric vehicles, so it is true to say that this firm were always very go-ahead in their trade.

William also had a good partner in life with his wife Ada, and they produced a son and a daughter. James, who was born in 1918, also followed in the family flourprints, and after undergoing an apprenticeship with Lowman's of Southampton in baking and catering, he returned to Hardway full of new ideas and enthusiasm. But war intervened, and young James was drafted into the R.A.F., where he was taught to deal with explosives. He laughingly describes his war service as "Going from buns to bangs, and back again"!

Father William was very much involved in the towns, affairs, he served on the Gosport council for many years, representing the Hardway ward. He was also on the Hampshire County Council, the local Hospital Board, as well as being a Justice of the Peace. But he paid the price for all his good deeds, and in 1945 he emulated his father by dying at the age of 56.

So James had a sad homecoming from the war, plus the fact that the Chapel Street bakery had been badly bombed, and had to be rebuilt. It is interesting to note that during the war,

"For those who will have the Best".
Ayling's Hardway Bakery.

in towns that had been badly blitzed, the consumption of bread soared. And so, with the war over, people had the taste for more bread, and James Ayling made sure they got it.

New branches of Ayling's bakery shops opened up all over the area, including Fareham and Lee-on-the-Solent. Business leaped fantistically, from an annual turnover in 1945 of £30,000, to £120,000 by 1951, employing a staff of over 100 workers. This is where the information about the Swiss Cafe I mentioned previously comes in, not many people realize that Ayling's owned this famous restaurant at one time.

In 1951, Ayling's were bought out by the giant Rank organization. They had also taken over Green's Bakery in

16

Bournemouth, they kept this name going, and so Ayling's became Greens Bakery. Of course, this bakery still flourishes from their headquarters at the Hardway.

The old shop in St. Thomas's Road, where it all started for the Ayling bakery empire, was taken over for a number of years by Lockyer's the grocers, but it has since been demolished and the site occupied by a row of modern town houses.

The old bakers were always very competitive, Cooper's proudly displayed adverts for their "Gold Medal Bread", while Roger's in North Street were more elaborate with "Roger's Bread, Sweetest and Best". The Ayling's combated this with "For those who will have the best".

But no matter what they said about their produce, the public could seldom complain, it always tasted fresh and tasty, even if it was produced in conditions that modern health inspectors would throw a blue fit over. Somehow, bread has never tasted the same since those days of our youth. Maybe our taste buds have changed, still, I hope you have enjoyed this chapter relating to some of the old Gosport bakers who "Gave Unto Us Our Daily Bread".

CHAPTER THREE

"One Man's Meat, Is Another Man's Living"

Years ago, getting the Christmas bird always seemed one of the great highlights of the festive season, but in these modern times all it entails is ordering one in advance from the butcher, than either putting it into your own freezer, or collecting it from the butchers frozen store a few days before the great day.

But in the old days, everything seemed to have been left to the last minute, with the turkey arriving on the kitchen table for preparation, sometimes not before midnight on Xmas Eve. This heralded the moment for our Mum and Auntie Flo to attack the poor deceased creature with great gusto, producing its innards with fiendish glee like female Doctor Frankensteins.

Dad and Uncle Arthur at this point would retire to the front parlour for a glass of brown ale, their task had been in buying and bringing home the bird from the market. Now that part was really exciting, for markets such as Charlotte Street on the eve of Christmas were a sight to behold, happy crowds jostling around the hurricane lamp illuminated stalls, the stall owners indulging in witty repartee with those amassed around them. Yes, it had an atmosphere all its own.

The butchers would auction off the meat and poultry, now the longer you could hang on, the cheaper it would get as the night went on. Hence the late arrivals home on Xmas Eve, or in fact any Saturday night.

Do you remember, how at holiday times the butchers and fishmongers would hang the poultry outside their establishments, sometimes stacked in rows right up to the top of the building. When choosing, there was always the temptation to ask for a bird that was on the top row!

As you may gather, the subject in this chapter concerns meat and fish, I shall combine the two, as many fishmongers sold poultry as well. Through the years Gosport could certainly boast of harbouring quite a number of these establishments, so let me see if I can conjure up some more names from the past.

They liked their meat back in the 1800's, in the middle part of that century there was at least sixteen butchers within the towns ramparts alone. Seven operated from the High Street, end even that narrow thoroughfare know as Bemisters Lane housed two butches shops. John Sweetman had his shop at No. 2 Bemisters Lane, and by the early part of this century it still supplied the same goods, under the auspices of Mr. August Rieffel, a well known pork butcher. At that time there was another pork butcher in Bemisters down at No. 14, this was Edward Smith. But 50 years before this in 1860, No. 14 had been the butchery establishment of a Mr. William George Harvey. Next door at No. 12, was the scene of operations for one of Gosport's most renowned family butchers, I will feature them a little later in this chapter, although I am sure most of you will know who I refer to by now.

Not too far away from Bemisters Lane, in Chapel Row there was a butcher named John Jones, this was in the 1850's. Now John was always shouting how good his meat was, and nobody could shout much louder than him, for he was in fact the Town Crier of Gosport in those days.

Things looked pretty bleak for Christmas dinners in 1870, there was a meat crisis, and prices leaped sky-high. Beef was 11d. a pound, and the cost of a turkey was 15/-! A lot of money in those days. But, it is worth noting that that splendid organization known as the Thorngate Trust, still delivered beef and plum pudding to the poor folk of the town that Christmas.

Around the turn of this century, Gosport must have looked very much like one of those Wild West cattle towns at times. I always chuckle when I think about the story my old friend George Foster told me about those days, this was when they had cattle drives right up the High Street. Boats looking more like landing barges would draw up to the Hard, then rural looking gents dressed in smocks and breeches, true farm yokel style, would herd the cattle out of the vessel and onto the waterfront. They would then drive the animals up the main street, dropping off at the various butchers or slaughter houses with the required order of beef or sheep. As Big John Wayne would have said: Herd 'em up, move 'em out!

Many older readers will remember the name of George Cox, he had shops in the High Street at No. 102 and 131. Both these sites had been the premises for butchers in the last century, notably Daniel Monk and Philip White. George Cox carried on his business in Gosport for over 50 years, he had a slaughter house in South Street where the animals spent their last hours before being killed for consumption by meat lovers.

Cox's were fond of advertising their Prime Devon Ox Beef, and South Down Wether Mutton. George was a true character, and was sorely missed when he died in 1939 at the age of 83.

George Foster also recalled Bob Bastin, another popular butcher who used to keep cattle to wait for slaughter on a piece of land near the old ramparts, penned in by iron railings. The Conservative Club has stood on this site since 1914. Bastin actually had two shops in North Cross Street, one at No. 12, and the other at No. 15, and it was at the latter that he specialized in dairy fed pork.

Another meat name that will ring a bell is that of W. & R. Fletcher, for at one time they had four shops in Gosport, one in the High Street where a Chinese restaurant now stands next to the electricity showrooms, one in Stoke Road, and two in Forton Road. Fletcher's developed quite a chain of butchers shops, with branches all over Portsmouth and Southampton.

"I'll have the one off the top please!"
Jack Colbern's fish and poultry shop, Stoke Road.

Forton Road shop of Thomas Moody.

If you went into the butchers shop of Barratt and Son in Stoke Road you would have to have nerves like steel, for the proprietor, a stocky gent with a beard, had an alarming habit of bringing down his chopping knife on the counter, missing customers noses by a hairsbreath if they got too close. Mr. Barratt had three sons, two of these in the form of Wallace and Ashby worked in the family business, while Ralph the third son became an engineer. He also had two daughters, and one of these married Mr. Magnell the old Gosport Town Clerk.

Still in Stoke Road, not far from Barratt's, on the corner of the 'Royal Arms' passage we had the shop of butcher William Burrows, and not much further up the road Maurice Pearman wielded his carving knife. So Stoke Road was very well catered

for in the way of butchers, not forgetting that Richard Moody had a shop at No. 113, but this was later taken over by Pearman's. Richard Moody also had another branch at 69, Forton Road, not to be confused with Thomas Moody the butcher, who was at No. 93. By the way, the rare and excellent photograph of Thomas Moody outside his shop in Forton Road was very kindly sent to me by his eldest daughter, Mrs. Edith Carrington, who is lucky enough to live in Santa Monica, sunny California.

Many readers by now will be saying to themselves, when is he going to mention the Withers family? Of course, no story about Gosport Butchers would be complete without saying something about this popular chain of family butchers, and I am very pleased to report that they are still carrying out their trade in the town, and carrying on the family tradition.

William Alfred Withers opened his first shop in 1910, this was in Chapel Street, off South Street. But within a couple of years he had moved premises to Bemisters Lane, in fact on the same site that they still operate from today.

Meat had to be brought over from Greetham Street in Portsmouth, and William did this by going across the ferry with a handcart to collect it, but later on he borrowed the money to get himself a horse and cart. William married Charlotte Jones, whose father was a well known Pompey butcher in Charlotte Street, known by one and all as 'Boner Jones'. William and Charlotte had five sons and three daughters, a lot of mouths to feed in those days. No doubt they were all meat-eaters!

In 1924 William opened another branch out in the country at Hardway. Well, it was out in the country then. A branch in Stoke Road followed in 1928, and this was followed by the Anns Hill premises in 1930. So four shops formed the chain, all nicely spread out to serve the community. All five sons entered the butchery trade, but Bill the eldest boy later left the trade. This resulted in his four brothers each running their own branch, Doug at Bemisters Lane, Jim at Anns Hill, Charlie in Stoke Road, and Frank at the Hardway Shop.

Father William continued to oversee his little butchery empire, and in fact was still buying meat for the shops at the age of 77. He died at the age of 87, in 1973, leaving the business in the hands of his four competent sons. And just as his Charlotte had helped him in his work, every one of the four brothers wives also helped in each of their shops.

In the old days they did not have the luxury of freezers in butchers shops, so ice was purchased at 1/6d. a hundredweight to lay the meat on. In Gosport's yachting heyday, the Withers supplied meat to many of the famous yacht owners and personalities that were moored in the harbour. Jack Hulbert and Cecily Courtneidge, Dorothy Paget the racehorse owner, and even some of the early submarines, they all had meat from the Withers organization.

And how about the price of that meat, some of the price tickets that Jim and Frank showed me from the 1930's made quite hilarious reading! Four filllet steaks cost 1/6d., four lamb chops at 7d., and 1lb of tender steak cost 10d.!

Within the past few years, after 50 years trading, Frank had to close the Hardway shop, retiring through ill health. And I am afraid Jim at Anns Hill has passed away, but the shop has been taken over by Doug's son Paul, so it is still a family business. Long may they flourish!

Before getting away from butchers in Gosport, here are a few more names that some older readers may remember. Eastmans, Booker, Burrige, Cooper, Hammond, Horne, Hale, Diment, Hayward, Jay, Helms, West, Vote, House, Sprules, New, and Parker. And that is really only the tip of the iceberg, but I hope I have sparked off a few memories for some of you. One thing is certain, we will never see steak at 10d. a pound again!

That does not quite finish this chapter, for if you remember I promised at the beginning to briefly touch upon fishmongers in the town, for they also dealt in poultry. There does not seem to be the amount of fish shops about nowadays, at least not like the old shops used to be, they were always open at the front without windows as such, and used to close their shops by pulling great shutters down. Being open like this they were awfully cold places to work in during the Winter time, having to handle the cold fish that were laid on the marble slabs could not have helped.

Most fishmongers now seem to have covered-in fronts with windows, our modern hygiene regulations have stopped foods such as meat and fish being openly displayed. Mind you, back

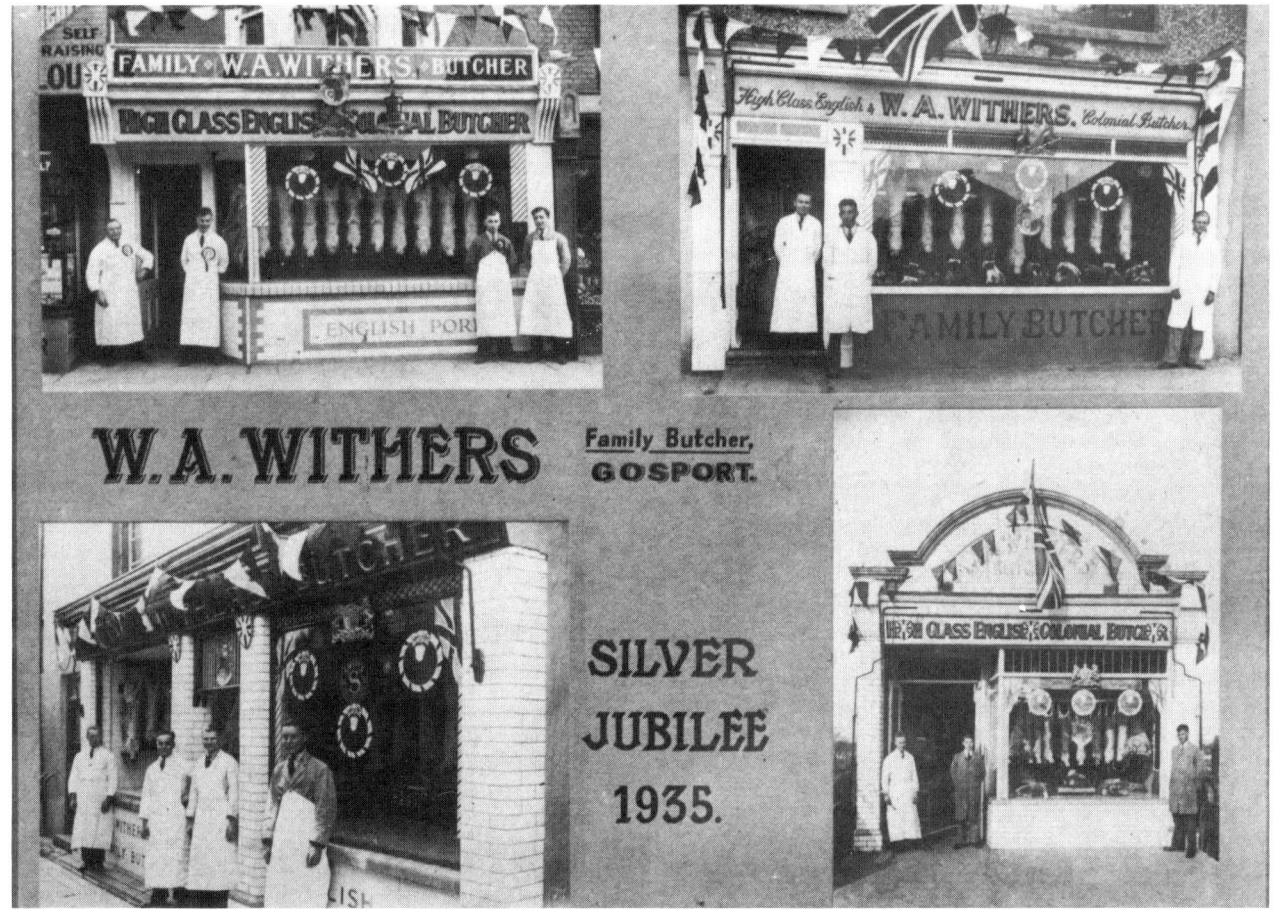

A quartet of Withers.
Top — Stoke Road and Anns Hill.
Lower — Bemisters Lane and Hardway.

in the early part of this century some folk were hygiene minded in Gosport, in fact there were a number of complaints about the great health hazzard in the High Street. What was this terrible hazzard? Well, believe it or not, it turned out that this was caused through the High Street shopkeepers themselves, their crime being that at 7 to 8 o'clock each morning they would shake their doormats into the public thoroughfare, thus spreading dust. Gee Whizz, you would be lucky now if you could find a shop open at that hour in the morning!

But I digress, back to fish. You have heard of the expression: 'Let them eat cake!' in the last century it was a case of: 'Let them eat fish' on one occasion. This was in the year 1800, a great scarcity of provisions was experienced in Gosport, it was so bad that a fund was raised to collect £900, the money was then used to purchase Scotch herrings to alleviate the peoples suffering.

In that century I have records of at least four fishmongers within the town, there was Henry Ridout and Thomas Shirvell in the High Street, Bill Johnson on The Green and the fourth was John Embling in North Street, Upfield's the drapers were later to take over this particular site at No. 87.

Leaping on 50 years or so, we shall have a reminder of some of the more familiar names in the fishmonger world. On the corner of Ashby Place in the High Street, there was a fish monger named Cook, and during the 1930's the shop was used for the same purpose by Miss F. Damon, this would be where Ruff's clock shop is now.

A few doors away, next to the old Gosport Theatre picture house, the well known fish business of Mr. A. E. Hooper was sited. Before readers start exclaiming "Oh, no it was'nt" in the best pantomime tradition, let me exclaim that this was in 1914, and a number of years later into the 1930's Hooper's moved down the High Street close to the South Cross Street corner,

and that is the shop that most people will have stronger memories of.

It is worth noting that Hooper's old shop next to the cinema, was taken over by Dorothy Cooper's ladies hat shop, I hope they managed to get rid of the rather strong smell of fish! This aspect does in actual fact bring back memories for me, at one time I worked in a High Street shop myself, and I remember that when the manager from Hooper's fish shop came in to settle their account, he would pay in notes taken out of his till. Need I state that these notes emitted a rather pungent smell that in turn pregnated our own till, resulting in my customers giving me rather strange looks for the rest of the day!

But back to the Hooper's of the 1930's, those days are well remembered by Jack Eales, who in turn will also be remembered for his services to the town as Mayor of Gosport. After a spell in the Merchant Navy, Jack came to Gosport in 1932 to manage Hooper's Gosport branch, for they had another shop at that time in Albert Road in Southsea. Jack did so well for the firm, that before long he became a managing director, and this was while he was still just a young chap. By the start of the war, Jack Eales was secretary for the towns Chamber of Trade, of which he was later made president. During that period he was involved in the difficult years of rationing, plus the fact that he was co-opted onto the Council, and I am pleased to say that he carried on in the post-war years, then in 1953 he put on the Mayor's mantle.

From Hooper's we will just pop across the road to North Cross Street, for it was there at No. 3 that Peter Arnett had his fish shop, by the way, No. 3 had previously been Lipton's grocery store. Arnett's were famous for their fish trade over in dear old Charlottee Street, then in 1925 they decided to open a branch in Gosport, and of course in their best tradition, they opened with a great sales raza-mataz. Great posters proclaimed for the opening: "Bring Big Bags and Baskets, But Little Money"!

At times you did not need money at all, this very often occurred on a Saturday night, with Frank Arnett giving away fish that was unsold to the poor folk of the area. But this was how trouble started, with Frank ending up in court. One evening at the close of business, his free fish giveaway attracted so many people that the road was blocked. P.C. Seamark took note of this, and estimated that there was about 90 people outside the North Cross Street shop, and after a warning, he booked Frank for causing an obstruction. I am pleased to say that our fishmonger friend was told-off by the magistrate for being a naughty boy, warned that he must not do it again, and fined 4/- costs! As I have always said: "There is something fishy in the State of North Cross Street"!

Stoke Road certainly had its fair share of fishmongers, in the early part of the 1900's Bill Hann had his shop at No. 11, but by the 1930's it had been taken over by Jack Colbern. In due course it was taken over by his son Ron, who retired fairly recently, but the shop still flourishes under the name of Colborn on the facia. Further down Stoke Road we had Elliott's fish shop at No. 73 and going down just past the Stone Lane junction was the shop of John Gard.

We must not confuse the name of Gard with Scard, for indeed Henry Scard had his fishmongery in North Street. In fact, Henry represented the fish trade on the food control committee that was set-up during the Second World War by the Chamber of Trade.

On the final round-up on fishmongers of the past, I will throw in the names of Bill Edwards and Bill Joyce, who both had fish shops in Forton Road, Jim Taylor had his in Whitworth Road, there was Walter Moxham in Henry Street, Percy Andrews in Alver Road, George Taw in Stoke Road, and finally Harold Rees in the High Street. I think that is enough to keep most fish-lovers happy.

You will no doubt notice that I have not as yet mentioned fried fish and chip shops, and as far as Gosport is concerned there was certainly enough of them, the list seems endless and I have no wish to bore you on the subject, so I will bow gracefully out on fish and chip shops. Having said that, I will keep my old R.M.L.I. friend Harry Camfield happy by mentioning Jenner's fish and chip shop near the old Forton Barracks, where many a marine went in for a pennyworth-of-each on the way back to barracks. Not so old readers will remember this same establishment better under the name of William Attwell, who became the proprietor before the last war.

Before the magic pills took over, to assist in the treatment of ulcers, many doctors would suggest a light diet, generally of fish and milk. Well, we have had the fish course, so for the next part of our diet of milk and nostalgia, turn to the next chapter.

CHAPTER FOUR

"Churning Things Over"

It seems to me that the 'Idiots Lantern' that stands in the corner of most of our living rooms, and the advertising media in general, goes to great lengths to get the message over about how good milk is for us, and about how marvellous its nutritional value is. I don't think anyone would disagree with this, in the less affluent days of yesteryear, I feel it was very often the only real protein that many youngsters got. That is why it is a shame that the practice of giving schoolchildren milk in the mornings has died out, although there are a few councils in the country that still manage to supply the kids with it, generally it has been discontinued.

Of course, when young we did not always realize how good it was for us, and although some did not particularly like drinking it, they had to gulp it down under the eagle eye of the teacher. Teachers knew it was good for us, do you remember how some of them on cold winter mornings used to put the milk bottles around the heating radiators to warm-up?

In earlier times we did not have the luxury of having our milk delivered in bottles, folk left their jugs outside the house, and when the milkman came along he would ladle the milk into the receptacles from the copper churn on his cart. Also the householder did not have the advantage of a modern refrigerator, so very often the milkman made two deliveries a day, one early in the morning, and the other later in the afternoon.

This practice could make the business of getting your daily pinta a trifle hazardous at times, especially at the weekend. Drunks would turn out of the pubs on a Friday or Saturday night, and while staggering home, if they felt the call of nature they would fill the jugs that had been left out with a liquid for which they were never intended. On dark mornings the milkman would ladle out the milk regardless from his churn, so therefore it is understandable that the customers first cup of tea in the day, had a rather distinctive flavour!

Do you remember how marvellous those old horses were that pulled the milkcarts, they appeared to know the rounds better than the milkman, clopping along gently to the next house while the milkman was delivering milk to another. Of course, they always had the sense to stop longer outside a house where they knew the customer would come out and feed them a sugar cube. The modern practice of electric or motor delivery vans is okay, but they cannot provide the useful bi-product that the old horses gave, resulting in keen gardeners going down the street armed with a bucket and shovel, the prize being that they produced some of the best roses in the neighbourhood!

So let us have a look at some of the dairy concerns of old Gosport, it is rather difficult now to imagine, but little more than fifty years ago the town was surrounded by green pastures, with cows contentedly chewing the cud. Needless to say, most of those fields have been filled in by houses. One of those green paradises for cows was sited at Bury Cross, this was behind where the Co-op supermarket is now sited, and it was known as Bury Grange Dairies. Those days are fondly remembered by 82 yr. old Kate Pigott, who after her education at St. Matthews School, joined Bury Grange to take over a milk round from a Miss Osgood. As Kate Savage, her maiden name, she would leave her home in Market Row near the old Green in Gosport at four o'clock in the morning to walk to the dairy just past the Rookery in Bury Road.

Kate delivered milk around the Alverstoke and Clayhall areas mostly, and recalls how peaceful and rural it all seemed in those days. It was fairly hard work for a young girl, and she

The start of a milk empire.
John Dyer on three wheels.

was always glad when her brother Walter was able to help her on the round. Although Kate confesses that she was terrified of cows, she loved her delivery horses, especially Big Joe, and a little chestnut horse who went under the name of Baby. There was also an older horse named Kit, who in the end got too old for the job and had to be shot. Needless to say, Kate and Walter cried for days!

Bury Grange Dairies had a shop in the High Street on the corner of Bemisters Lane, where Bateman's the opticians now operates. But most of their milk was sold over in Southsea, this was because Charlie House appeared to have the milk monopoly in Alverstoke. Charles Henry House, to give his full title, certainly commanded a vast expanse of farmland to the north of the area, including Privett, Grange, Rowner and Lee-on-the Solent.

Charles certainly had plenty of energy, as well as keeping an eye on his farm holdings, his two sons Phillip and Maurice, and the Hambledon Hunt, he also served on the Gosport District Council, the Fareham Rural District Council, and was churchwarden at Rowner Church from 1899 to 1934. In actual fact, 1934 was the year he died, aged 74.

Charles Kennard came to Gosport in 1906, he also was very energetic, and had a very shrewd business brain, this allowed him to build one of the most successful dairy firms in the town. He was very forward thinking, and by 1922 he had installed at his Stoke Road premises some of the most up-to-date equipment that could be obtained at that time. Older readers may remember Kennard's dairy shop on the corner of Jamaica Place later to be taken over by another well known dairy name, Dyer's of course. I am afraid Charles Kennard did not live to see his milk empire grow, for he died in 1923 aged 50.

Another dairy name from the past was sited at the beginning of the High Street, at No. 1 was the premises known as Perkins Dairy. Mrs. Perkins was the driving force behind this concern, and was associated with Gosport High Street for most of her life, being born at No. 31. In 1865 she married Edwin Perkins, an Isle of Wight farmer, they moved to Gosport to open a dairy at No. 107 High Street, this was in 1893. Edwin died in 1895 leaving his good lady to carry on the business, this she did with great gusto, first moving to No. 139, and later to those premises at No. 1 in the High Street.

Mrs. Perkins was a hard worker, and apart from her support for the Congregational Church across the road, she had very little social life. She retired in 1919, leaving the management of the dairy to her son Fred, she died 10 years later.

In the early part of this century, another formidable lady in the form of Fanny Cobb had a flourishing dairy business in the heart of the village of Alverstoke in Coward Road. She was followed on that site in later years by Wilf Jerome, whom many older village folk will recall from the pre-war days for his milk supplies.

Out at Brockhurst we had the Brockhurst Dairies run by the Sheppard Brothers, while in Brockhurst Road William Goodenough had his dairy. Poor old Bill ran foul of the weights and measures inspector a few times I am afraid, in 1926 he was found guilty of defrauding the public by selling milk 9% deficient in non-fatty solids, and was fined £25, this being the dairies third offence.

Martin was a popular dairy name in Gosport, with dairies in Seahorse Street, Stoke Road, Mount Street, and Kings Road. In Forton Road Harry Holding had his shop in between Russell and Durham Streets, but the name that will be better remembered in Forton is the dairy of William Cathery, not far from the corner of Park Road. After William died the dairy was run by Kate Cathery, we must not confuse William with Charles Cathery, who had a grocery shop further down Forton

Road, on the corner of Victoria Street.

Venturing towards Elson, we must not forget the Slocombe Dairy in Melville Road, and into the Hardway area we had Messrs. Hoare and Dumbrill, at one time Hoare and Edney. But of course, out at Hardway we had the best known Gosport Dairy of them all, founded by James Dyer, it just grew and grew. Until recent times Dyer's Dairy more or less shared the monopoly of milk supply in Gosport along with the Co-op, then they became part of the giant Tom Parker dairy concern, and although the vans have 'Tom Parker' emblazoned on them, I still think of them as 'Dyers Dairy'. Anyway, Parker's still use the Priory Road works where it all started.

Before I wind up Gosport's milk connections, I know I shall get into trouble if I do not mention Stoddard's Dairy in Stoke Road, run by John Stoddard, then later by Fred Stoddard. If you remember, this dairy was on the corner of Prince Alfred Street near the approach to Gosport Road Station, alas, now gone.

Although I have only mentioned milk, many establishments also sold other dairy produce, such as eggs, butter and cheese. Regarding eggs, in those days although they were available in dairy shops, it is a fact that most folk kept their own hens in the back yard. Of special mention is the hen that belonged to Mr. Bull of Alver Road, in 1907 she distinguished herself by laying an abnormally large egg, it weighed 5¼ ozs., and measured 7½ inches around the middle, and a length of 8½ inches. Ouch!

If you think that was unusual, how about the Gosport hen that underwent a sex change? The bird belonged to Mr. G. Miller of Park Road, hatched in March 1924, between November of that year and November of 1925 it laid over 200 eggs. Then it ceased to lay, certain sex peculiarities were noticed, the bird began to crow, adopt the actions of a male, and develop a large comb and wattles, plus neck hackles and tail feathers of a male. But in the following year after a moult, the plumage of a female returned, although it retained its spurs. Undoubtedly, a very strange case indeed!

Before we draw away from food supplies, and deal with other types of traders in the town, you may have notied that I have not mentioned greengrocers. The reason for this is that many provision grocers also sold fruit and veg, in fact many of them sold anything and everything that could pull in a profit. having said that, I would not like to leave out characters such as Albert Lockyer who started at the Hardway, George Wall, who had several shops in the town, or Harold Wiltshire from Bemisters Lane, for they all specialized in greengrocery, as did many more, but space does not permit me to mention them all.

Gosport High Street.
Cory's Coach Works next to Woolworth's 3d and 6d Stores.

28

CHAPTER FIVE

"Clothes Maketh The Man, And Woman"

When people start talking about the clothes that they have bought in the past, it is inevitable that the 'Fifty-bob Taylor' will crop up. Yes, it is true, I can verify to younger readers that you really could buy a suit for £2.50p., and jolly good they were too! Of course, this was in the days when everyone had a best suit for Sundays, no matter what you wore in the week, Sunday was the day for dressing up. This was very much influenced by the fact that most people went to church that day, as yet they were pure innocents that had been untouched by the lure of such distractions as television, or the cinema, for picture houses were not allowed to open on the Lord's Day.

When the clothes were trundled out of the wardrobes for outings such as this, or for funerals, what always made a deep impression on me was the strong smell of mothballs that filled the air. It is strange, but the mothball aroma is a particular smell, we very seldom come across nowadays, perhaps it is because people seem to wear their best clothes all week now, and on Sundays they jump into casual wear. One might also form the opinion that modern insecticides have indeed vastly depleted the poor old moth!

It was far easier years ago to distinguish a persons class through his clothes, it was generally accepted that the well-to-do gent always wore a topper or bowler hat, the middle-class tradesman usually wore a trilby or perhaps a straw boater, while the working chap nearly always had a cloth cap pulled down over his ears. As I said, it is not so easy now, with our more affluent society some of the chaps digging holes in the road look as if they have stepped out of Burton's window. I suppose with all the wonderful machinery available now, they hardly get their clothes dirty!

Talking of Burton's, they came to Gosport just before the war in 1939, the building being quite outstanding for the High Street at that time, the architecture looked upon as very futuristic. But we shall be looking back before that particular period, and having a reminder of some of the mens and ladies clothing establishments that flourished in earlier times. I will also throw in drapery concerns for good measure, so put in your order for a yard of elastic now, while stocks last!

It is interesting to note that there was at least twenty tailors and outfitters cutting and sewing within the towns ramparts in the 1850's, half of those were sited in the High Street, whilst the remainder had their premises in the side streets, such as Chapel Row, King Street, Northcross and Southcross Streets.

From that period there is an establishment that is worth noting, this was at No. 112 High Street, parading under the banner of Woodrows and Rowe, tailors and hatters. This was the site taken over by George Cooke and subsequent provision shops, until it once again reverted to tailoring when Burton's opened on that same spot, turning a complete circle as it were.

That name Rowe is also interesting, this was the start of the famous tailoring family that was to make such a mark on Gosport's commercial world. Within twenty years William Rowe had struck out on his own, and by 1878 he was well established as a naval outfitter and contractor, operating from No. 78 in the High Street, with branches at Portland and Sheerness.

Older residents of the town will have memories of his son who took over the firm, he was another William, and he was a well known Gosport character, strutting around the town with an enormous cigar in his mouth. If anyone had the image of a prosperous business man, then it was certainly William Rowe.

Burt's for buttons and bows. 1912.

The Rowe establishment had a large work force, and through the years provided plenty of employment for the town. Amongst the tailors working there were Bill Edmunds, Bill Millard, Joe Potter, Sid Smith, Mr. Workman, and Mr. Hocking. Also, we must not forget Ron Lawson who was in charge of the counter staff in the front shop.

William Rowe was a bachelor and lived with his sister in Bury Road. He served as a local magistrate for 24 years, also on the Hampshire County Council, and was very high in free-masonry circles. I might add that his great passion outside these activities was pigeon racing. William died in 1936 at the age of 78, and the tailoring establishment became Harris & Parkin.

Still in the High Street, in the region near Bemisters Lane, there flourished a very old Gosport name in the provision and making of clothes and also in the world of drapery, that name was Blake. Back in the 1850's John Garson Blake had the corner site upon which Bishops the shoe and outfitting store, and Boots the Chemists are now trading on.

By the 1870's he had been joined by George Blake, and they extended to take in 110 High Street, along with 108 and 109. In the early 1900's the two latter numbers were in the name of George Blake, linen drapers and ladies outfitting, whilst the men were catered for by Henry Blake next door at No. 110.

In Henry Blake's tailoring establishment in 1910 you could buy a Harris Tweed smart winter overcoat for the princely sum of 32/6d., and if you required a shirt, the choice was yours at 3/6d., 4/6d., 5/6d., or if you were really loaded you might splash out on a good quality shirt for 7/6d.! It is worth noting that if you required a shirt to be made to measure, the price range started from 4/6d.! But folk were rather thrifty in those days, so Blake's provided a service in which they reconditioned shirt collars and cuffs for half-a-crown. Or if you prefer, 12½p.

Henry Blake also catered for the more well-to-do client, and a good selection of gentlemens shooting, golf, and riding breeches could always be found on his shelves. Henry carried on his business for many years, gents were still getting outfitted there into the late 30's, but George Blake's drapery empire had disappeared to make way for Bishops and Boots. Henry Blake's has also been long gone, but I am pleased to report that a menswear shop still operates at No. 110, this being Foster Brothers.

Bertrand Rodwell came to Gosport in 1912 to manage George Blake's drapery store, and when the business closed he opened up his own drapery and ladies undergarment shop

William Rowe's tailoring staff line-up for a jolly works outing.

down the High Street at No. 119. But his success was not long lived, for Bertrand died suddenly in 1925 at the age of 49, sadly missed at St. Matthews Church where he was a church-warden for several years.

Rowe's did not have it all their own way in their speciality of naval and military tailoring, they had healthy competition from Charles Gorman in North Street. Charles was much respected in the town, as was his wife, who until her death in 1898 was a Gosport postmistress. Charles died himself fourteen years later in 1912.

The military tailors in the area certainly enjoyed a good trade, for the New Barracks in Clarence Road attracted many famous regiments through the years. William Furlong was at least one chap who knew the secret of how the Guards and Cavalry Officers maintained their regal bearing. The answer was that they wore corsets! William was in the male corset business for over sixty years, making and designing the garments, and one particular item for which he was in popular demand was for making stays of pink silk and satin for the officers. I have always said 'There is something about a Soldier!'

Anyway, we shall be delving a little later into the subject of corsets, or the meat packing industry as it is sometimes referred to, but before that we shall be having a reminder about another couple of Gosport tailors. I am sure the name of Masterman will be familiar to many readers, for Henry Masterman was not only famous for his tailoring establishment at 95 and 96 the High Street, but also for the fact that he served as the Mayor of Gosport in 1924.

Henry Masterman was born in Portsmouth, but he came to Gosport in 1882 to start his business. It was a large impressive shop, both inside and out, for on top of the buildings front were three rather distinctive spires, they can in fact still be seen. Henry soon made his mark on the town, both in business, and in the towns affairs. He was elected to the Urban District Council in 1921, and was prominent as a magistrate.

It was just as well that Henry was not sitting up on the Bench in 1926 when a chap arrested for drunkeness was brought before the court, rather the worse for drink he had staggered up the High Street, pausing only to throw a brown paper parcel at a shop window. The window of Masterman's.

This was rather unfortunate, for the parcel had a iron shoe-makers last inside it! Henry's son Gordon was serving at the time, and one can imagine his surprise at this special delivery via the window. A constable appeared on the scene as if by magic, and began questioning the inebriated parcel thrower.

The officer in blue asked him if he knew that the shop window was the property of the Mayor of Gosport, to which the drunken culprit replied rather ungraciously: "Whoooosh eee, when eee's at home?" No doubt he soon found out when he had sobered up! Henry Masterman died in 1927 aged 69.

Chaps, can you remember the struggle we had to fit those stiffly starched collars to our separate shirts? This might explain why men in earlier times always had a ruddy expression on their faces, they were in actual fact choking! When the wearing of shirts with attached collars became popular, think of all the stud manufacturers that went broke.

I recall that the last separate collar that I bought was at Hart & Co., the North Cross Street mens outfitters. Montague Hart was a great character in the town, he had founded the business in 1884. He was a very shrewd man to deal with when conducting business, so you will not be surprised to learn that he was a very prominent member of the Portsmouth Jewish community. Anyway, when he died in 1934, he left £19,000 and that was a great deal of money in those days.

Before we switch onto more delicate fabrics, if you want a good laugh why don't you get your old wedding photographs from out of the sideboard. Mine are real corkers, the suit I was wearing, not made in Gosport I might add, makes me look a cross between Richard the Third, and the Hunchback of Notre Dame!

Right, laughbreak over, now we are going to give the ladies a fashionable turn. I have found in my investigations that the chief essentials for female apparel in the last century appeared to relate to two garments, a good pair of corsets, and a pretty hat.

As far as the latter article of clothing was concerned, in the mid-1800's Gosport town could boast a good array of milliners, in fact no less than eleven such establishments. I find some of the proprietors names rather charming, top of this list must be Amelia Softley who worked from Haslar Street, whilst in Forton we could have obtained our bonnets from Miss Emma Silverlock. But of course in later years, the number of hat shops appeared to be vastly depleted, and it came down really to only one prominent name in this particular field, that of Dorothy Cooper in the High Street, her windows crammed with what appeared to the male eye as all kinds of strange and funny looking headgear creations. Cooper's left the High Street in the early 1970's, and it is rather nice in a way that the feminine tradition has been kept, for the shop is now in use by a ladies fashion store, that of Joy Nicholson. Readers may recall that Nicholson's had their shop further up the High Street opposite the Post Office at one time, and though one hears of 'closing down' sales, Nicholson's were unique in the fact that they had a 'falling down' event. This occurred when building work was in progress either side of their fashion shop, the doors were shut one Wednesday at 1 o'clock for half-day closing and ten minutes later the building collapsed completely! I kept telling them not to slam the doors too hard!

Now it could be said that corset manufacturers were living off the fat of the land! On the same score, I suppose the same thing could be said about the people who sold them, and I should also think that the establishment of James Oliver Upfield would also have a strong challenge for that dubious title. So ladies, please draw in a deep breath when I reveal that in 1910 Upfield's were selling genuine English made whale-bone corsets for 1/11½d. a pair.

In those Edwardian days, the Victorian passion for wearing corsets was still very much with us, and through many an open window could be heard the sound of squelching flesh as maids pulled with great gusto on two cords whilst at the same time having two feet firmly implanted in madam's back! You see

Upfield's in North Street.

what I mean by meat-packing!

James Oliver Upfield took the family drapery business over from his father, who had originally founded it in 1859. To keep up the tradition, when James himself retired in 1924 his two sons took it over from him, and many readers will recall the two very tall Upfield brothers, always so courteous and helpful.

Those who ever entered Upfield's North Street emporium, will confirm what a glorious assortment of merchandise could be found on view, everything from colourful materials to needles and pins. It was also one of those stores that employed the overhead trolley system of transmitting cash back and forth to the prim and smartly dressed young lady who sat in a rear paydesk, your change would magically return the same way in the canister, and if the amount was as small as one farthing, you might get a packet of pins in lieu. If you recall, fishmongers were great users of the trolley system, but the change still smelt of fish!

James actually worked in the North Street store for over 50 years, and during his spare hours he served on the Urban District Council until it became a Borough in 1922. He was a founder member of the Rotary Club, and also of Lee-on-the Solent golf club, he died in 1935.

Meanwhile, back in Gosport High Street we must not miss Madame Shears dusting off her dummies in the window, Madame had a popular ladies outfitters next door to our old friend Henry Masterman. While on the other side of the road next to the Catholic Church was the drapery bazaar of another Henry, Henry Burt. This was quite a large store, with two floors parading under the title of the Clarence Drapery Arcade. Every inch of window space was crammed with merchandise, and Burt's illustrated brochures informed visitors that they had not seen all the attractions Gosport had to offer unless they had paid a visit to the Burt Bazaar.

Creeping up into Stoke Road, we must not forget the well loved drapery store of Andrew's, closed in fairly recent times. This was originally run by two spinster ladies the Misses L. & E. Andrews, it is quite amazing how many pairs of spinster sisters ran businesses, and it is a fact that they were either confectionery, drapery, or wool shops, and the most popular business for them to run appeared to be tearooms.

Over on the other side of Stoke Road, where Eric Cooper's antique shop is now sited on the corner of Holly Street, it is often forgotten that the Co-op also had a drapery department on that spot at one time, in fact during the 30's. Further along on the corner of Peel Road was the ladies outfitting shop of

Anne Crosland, and this particular establishment will bring back memories for many ladies.

I received a letter from Mrs. Joyce Hawkins who now lives in Plymouth, in which she tells me how as Joyce Coleman she remembers buyng her first bra at Crossland's. I must admit that I get frightened sometimes about this strange power I have over women, in which they are prompted to write and tell me about such intimate revelations. Anyway, Joyce remembers that the bra was a fine pink lawn material, with ribbon straps and a complicated cross-over arrangement of elastic at the back, coming round to fasten with two buttons at the front. As Joyce states, girls were not encouraged to 'accentuate the positive' in the 30's!

As you may imagine the list of ladies outfitting shops through the years could seemingly go on and on, but I will have to finish with just two more names, one from the distant past in the form of the High Street establishment of Marie et Cie, and the other which is a little more recent is the Stoke Road shop of Lillian Gent, who is in fact still flourishing from the corner of Alver Road.

So there you are, we are now dressed in the height of sartorial elegance, a smart hat, well tailored suit or dress, ready to anywhere. I say, I tell you what, you look really funny standing there with bare feet! Never mind, we can rectify that in the next chapter, but just give me a moment to get out of my Upfield's corset!

CHAPTER SIX

"Saving Soles"

Looking back to my school days, I recall that there was one thing most of the lads had in common, apart from the fact that we had dirty necks and finger nails, most of my pals had holes in the seat of their short trousers, or holes in the soles of our boots. The latter was generally caused through an enthusiasm for playing football on the hard playground, or on joining the stream of lads that would slide across the playground on icy winter mornings.

Until the boots could be repaired, the usual ploy was to line the insides with a piece of cardboard. Dad more often than not would try and repair the footwear himself, this resulted in most homes in the old days owning one of those three-legged iron contraptions known as cobblers lasts. It seems strange that those same iron lasts are quite collectable items to be found in antique fairs nowadays.

Dad would disappear into the shed with the offending boots, this was followed by a great deal of banging and tapping, and sometimes swearing! He would then return with the announcement: "There, that should do you for a while". Whereupon I would don the repaired boots, and immediately invent a new dance, thanks to the nails coming through the soles.

As I got older and bought my own shoes, I soon learnt to smuggle them into the house without Dad seeing them, for if he did he would grasp them in his banana-type fingers and start pulling them all over the place, akin to tearing a telephone directory in half. When satisfied, he would proclaim: "Yes, they seem strong enough", and hand the new shoes back to me, by now looking as if they were about two years old!

As I ventured out into the outside world after a shoe repairing session, the cry from Mum would be: "Now mind how you go up the kerbs". The reason for her concern was that I usually had about half-an-inch of leather overlapping the soles! So if you wanted your shoes properly repaired, the answer just had to be, go to a professional boot or shoe repairer.

There was certainly plenty of these tradesmen in the old days to go to, my directory for 1859 lists over 30 in the Gosport area. This was before the days of mass production, and boots and shoes were made by hand of course, with some of the hand-stitched made-to-measure shoes and boots for more wealthy customers involving many hours of labour for the cobbler.

Although I cannot possibly touch upon all of them, I will never the less try and provide a brief reminder of some of the better known businesses that made their living through handling leather.

One of the foremost names in the town relating to footwear, must be that of F. G. Nobes and Co. in Stoke Road, and although the business has undergone a few changes, the name is still proudly displayed on the facia. Back in the mid-1800's Frederick Nobes could be found stitching and hammering away in a small workshop in North Street, sometimes into the small hours. In the year 1868 a son was born into the Nobes family, he was also named Fred, and as he got older Fred Senior taught him the tricks of the shoe trade.

In between cutting leather and banging away with the happier, young Fred found time to marry a lovely girl named Martha Drover in 1890 at the Stoke Road Union Chapel. One year later a son was born to Fred and Martha, now guess what they named him that's right, Fred!

Fred and Martha expanded the business, at this particular time they were operating from No. 71 Stoke Road, a lovely old

Fred Nobes and Bert Asher outside the Old Shop in Stoke Road.

shop with the letters 'N' ornately engraved on the front windows. They provided a personal shoe service, for example, Gosport resident Winnie Sellers had Nobes make her a pair of green kid shoes for her wedding in 1908. Just think how much this kind of service would cost now!

Fred died at the age of 43 in 1911, and Martha carried on the business with the help of her son Fred, and a young chap named Bert Asher whom she brought into the shop. When the First World War had finished, with Fred and Bert returning from the forces, Martha retired and handed the business over to them. They managed to get through the following years of depression, and in fact expanded the trade even more by dealing in sports goods.

They moved to new premises a short step down the road in 1937, to Nos. 55 & 57 Stoke Road. By that time they had been joined by a young man named George Collett who specialized in sports goods, and when Nobes became a limited company in 1952 George was made a director. Fred Nobes died in 1971, and Bert Asher passed on in the following year.

George carried on until 1976, when Fred Nobes daughter Joan Leslie, took over with her husband Peter, thus keeping the family link going. But that link was finally severed in April of 1981, when Joan and Peter sold the business. I am pleased to say that the shop still deals in footwear and in sports goods, and that George Collett still pops in once a week to repair sports goods, and assist generally.

There is hardly any need for me to remind Gosport residents of the other well known name in the boot and shoe trade in the town, it just has to be that of the famous Mills family, a business that I am pleased to state is still flourishing. Many readers are familiar with the shop in Stoke, but not too many will recall the other branch of Mills in Clarence Road, founded in 1890 by Matthew Mills.

His son Fred was certainly a popular chap in the town, not only for his work skills in the shoe trade, but also for his sporting prowess as a boxer. This 'Fighting Cobbler' was a little marvel in the ring, and in his day he fought some of the best names in the game, and always gave a good account of himself. We must not forget that Fred had a younger brother named Pat, who was also a dab hand with the gloves on, in fact he became a professional and picked up titles all over the world.

Fred Mills once took part in an exhibition boxing match with the great European Champion Bugler lake, and it was noticeable that Fred was getting in some pretty nifty blows to the champs facial features. In fact at one stage he turned to the referee, who happened to be the legendary World Fly-weight Champion Jimmy Wilde, and said: "Look, who is giving this ruddy exhibition, him or me"?

Sadly, during the last war Fred Mills lost a leg during a bombing raid on Gosport, but this could not top a chap with his kind of determination, and he could be found at the Stoke Road shop cheerfully going about his cobbling trade. Fred died in 1969 at the age of 77. But I am pleased to say that his son John followed in his fathers footsteps, and has carried on the family tradition in Stoke Road. The Clarence Road shop has long since disappeared, along with most of the old Clarence and North Street areas.

But before we move away from Clarence Road it is worth remembering another leather association that it once had, this was through the saddle and harness business of Walter Morgan. Walter was born in West Meon, he came to Gosport in 1885 to work for Mr. Tyler the saddler in the High Street. He did so well he decided to go into business on his own account, and so opened his shop in Clarence Road in 1892. Walter stitched and cut away for over forty years there, until he retired in 1937. He was to die two years later in 1939 at the age of 73.

Not so very far away in North Street, Charles Small ran his leather business which he had opened when he first came to Gosport in 1890. Charles was a great character around the town, a staunch member of the Wesleyan Church in Stoke Road, and he was actually in the Gosport Volunteers when over 60 years old. Although Charles died in 1930 and his son Frank did not enter the world of leather, he would never the less have bery proud of his sons achievements, for Frank went into the teaching profession and made his mark at the old Clarence Square School under Mr. Coalbran, and later when he became headmaster of Grove Road School. Well loved by all his pupils and staff, Frank Small died recently in 1981 at the age of 91.

But back to footwear, you can see how easy it is to digress. There was a number of shoe repairers and makers in Stoke Road in addition to Mills, not so far away was shoemaker Reg Stock, and a bit further along was the shop of Alf Cole, next to where W. H. Smith's old shop used to be. But in the old days Forton Road just had to be the shoe-repairers mecca, see how many of the following you remember in Forton, Reg Goodall, Frank Everitt, Alex Chiverton, Albert Aldred, Sidney Arm, Edwin Briar, and Arthur Branton, just to name a few!

But back towards the High Street, I have already mentioned Bishops on the corner of Bemisters Lane, and I know I will be shot if I do not mention Len Taylor's shop in the Lane itself, Len also had another branch in Whitworth Road. The High Street boasted a good selection of shoe shops in those balmy pre-war days, as indeed it does today, names such as those of Freeman Hardy & Willis, Stead & Simpson, not forgetting the old established firm of Worley's, who originally started in Stoke Road.

I have space for just one more name from the shoe world, by now you will have guessed that I am going to say Corbin's in North Cross Street, for George Corbin's shoe shops were very popular, and long established in Portsmouth and Southsea. Just to give you an idea what we used to pay for our footwear, Corbin's in Gosport were advertising the sale of good sturdy mens shoes for 12/11d. a pair, whilst you could buy a pair of rubber Wellingtons for only 10/11d., this was in 1925. Ah, those were the days!

Well, there you are, you are now fully outfitted, and jolly smart you look too! Having a good suit in the old days was a great asset, if you were short of a bob or two you could always go to 'Uncles' and put it in pawn, our old friends from North Cross Street, Sidney Smith or Arthur Couzens, were always happy to oblige. Some of the suits at the old pawnshops went in and out more often than the tide!

CHAPTER SEVEN

"Scrub-a-Dub-Dub"

Do you remember those old 'Monday Washday Blues'? There was poor old Mum hunched over the boiler with a copper stick in her gnarled hands, absolutely sweating buckets of perspiration. Then it all had to be hung out in the back yard, propped up on the rope line with a long stick, thus allowing Dad's woolen 'long-johns' to flutter proudly in the breeze.

Next came the ironing, none of your thermostatically controlled gear then, the iron would be taken off the range and given a goodly dollop of spit to test its heat. My Mum had a tendency to starch everything with great abandon, turning your nect at the collar was bad enough, but the shirts were so stiff it made one move around like a stilted version of Frankenstein's monster!

My goodness, if our grandmothers and mothers could come back now and see all the fantastic equipment that the modern housewife has at her disposal, automatic washers, heated tumbler dryers, steam irons and spray starches, the poor old dears would think they were in clover to have had aids like this.

Of course, not everyone did their washing at home, the better-off members of the community would send their washing to a laundry. But these establishments were badly affected by the advent of the washing machine, or at least when the machines came into the financial reach of the working classes after the last war, plus that High Street invention known as laundrettes.

In earlier days we had a number of laundries around Gosport, and they enjoyed a good trade, despite a lot of moonlighting from the lady down the street who took-in other

The cleanest place in town.
Flux's Laundry, Haslar Street.

peoples washing. The laundries in fact did a good job by providing a great deal of employment for the ladies of the town, although I find there are a lot of folk who are not ready to admit that they or their mothers once worked in a laundry. I see no reason why not, it was a good honest way of earning a crust, especially when the main breadwinner of the family was perhaps out of work, you must put something on the table.

Let us have a reminder of a few Gosport laundries from the past, and I bet when I make a simple statement "Flux's Laundry", many readers will ender nods of recognition, for they were at one time a household name in the town. This laundry was in Haslar Street, and it had its main gate in that street, but it also had another gate leading into South Street.

The laundry site had originally been that of a brewery, and this was rather interesting, for it had its own water supply from an artesian well sited the building. Flux's had a workforce of about 100 people, and they were overseered by the manager, Mr. Taylor. His foreman was a chap named Joe Gomes, whose wife Esther was also a forewoman. Mr. Brown was the chief boiler stoker and maintenance man, and there was also a team of drivers with the names of Bosbury, Pickering, and Davis.

One of the laundries favourite characters was a dear old lady named Granny Tilbury, and I believe she had several daughters who worked there. Despite a flat wage of 7d. per hour, it was a happy-go-lucky place to work, and by the flickering gas lights the girls would have a jolly good sing-song to keep their peckers up, and thus get the work out on time. One establishment that was very pleased to have Flux's sited near them was Gillard's shop on the corner of Haslar Street, they sold everything from ham to hairpins, their greatest attraction being that they let the girls from the laundry have goods on the slate.

I hardly need to tell you that Flux's Laundry is no longer with us, and I am afraid neither is the next call on our laundry list, the Inverness Laundry in the road of the same name. This establishment was also to develop into a very large concern, all thanks to the hard work and determination of one lady, her name was Harriett Richards.

Just before the turn of the century Harriett lived in Brougham Street, she would bustle through the streets of Gosport collecting dirty washing, to take home and launder and then return it to the customer for what we might deem now a mere pittance. After a hard days washing you may imagine that Harriett was tired enough, and to lug a great basket around called for a special breed of woman. But it was not long before she was able to invest in her first collection and delivery vehicle, an old pram!

And so this formidable lady could be seen pushing around her spotless white load, recommendation spread by word of mouth and work poured in until it was obvious that she would need larger premises. Local builder John Rapley came to Harriett's aid, he suggested a possible site in nearby Inverness Road, and that is how the laundry came to take over Number One, Lansdowne Villas in 1902.

She started by taking on two girls, but it was not long before she had to increase her workforce. She also modernized her transport system, she bought a donkey and cart! The trouble was that the donkey had a mind of its own at times, if it wanted to move it did, and if it did not want to move it did'nt!

The business developed so rapidly that Harriett's husband Harry Richards left his bricklaying occupation and came to help in the laundry, they were also helped by their daughters Maude and Dorothy. And still the work flowed in, washing contracts for the Forton Marine Barracks, later St. Vincent, also for H.M.S. Dolphin and the War Memorial Hospital. The New Barracks was also on their rounds, notably for the King's Royal Rifles. Prince Maurice of Battenberg was so pleased with the service the laundry gave him, he presented Harriett with a special Royal lamp before the regiment left for foreign parts.

In 1925 Dorothy Richards married Charles White, and as her father Harry was suffering from bad health at the time, Charles joined the business to help out. He was to stay for 30 years, and eventually become managing director. The year 1938 was an important one in the history of the Inverness Laundry, a new building was constructed with much improved facilities. By this time the poor old donkey had long been pensioned off, the delivery fleet having expanded to four vans. Some readers may remember Fred Windmill, who drove for the firm for many years.

Inverness Laundry staff
Harriett Richards is second left in front row.

Mention of the latter sparks off more recent memories of their building, many will remember it in the 1960's, on the row of the Gosport Road hill leading down to Fareham's Lower Quay. The surrounding site has been demolished for road widening in recent years, ah! well, that's progress. Anyhow, Charles and Dorothy White are still living happily in retirement out in the peace of Swanmore, and well deserved it is too, after all those years of hard work, laundries of old were not the greatest of places to work in, especially in the summer.

The workforce of over fifty washed happily away, and for any lady reader who hates ironing, think how much they had to do in the old laundries. This the Inverness girls did by continuously relaying the hot irons from a great stove in the middle of the workroom. New methods and equipment made the job easier, but they also caused redundancy in the laundry business. Although by 1959, Inverness still employed 32 staff, and they handled 14,000 items of washing every week.

Charles and Dorothy retired in 1960, and their son David took over in partnership with Mr. Saville from the Lee White Laundry. But a few years later both the Inverness and the Lee laundries were to close down, swallowed into the Alverstoke and Fareham Laundry concern.

CHAPTER EIGHT

"Any Old Iron-monger"

"When Father painted the parlour, you couldn't see Pa for paint, dabbing it here, dabbing it there, dabbing it, dabbing it, everywhere"!

So went the words of the old song, and I could not think of anything better to describe the scene when my old Dad managed to get his hands on a paint brush! We used to hide them from him! Do you remember when green and cream paint was all the rage? I do, my Dad invented that craze, everything was green and cream, the walls, the ceiling, the floors, the gas stove, the rice pudding, and even old Mother Kelly's ginger tom from next door was splashed green and cream! A cat-astrophe!

To buy your paint years ago you usually went to a hardware or ironmongers store, they did not have the posh 'home decor' showrooms that we have today, if you wanted wallpaper you chose it out of a sample book and then they arranged to get it in for you, they did not have the space to keep large stocks.

Looking back, they did not have any space at all, just about everything under the sun was packed into those old hardware shops, right up to the ceiling. What they could not show inside had to go outside, I should think they had to start putting it all out about an hour before they opened, filling the pavement with a multitude of goods from dusbins to rolls of lino. Do you remember lino? It has all gone posh now, they call it floor covering! Anyway, before they closed for the night all the goods had to be brought back in, what a performance!

Many readers will still have fond memories of dear old Murphy's in North Street, no matter what you asked for there was always a good chance that amongst all those countless

Dear Old Murphy's in North Street, 1930's.

boxes and drawers they would find what you wanted. It was rather sad to see this revered establishment fall to the demolition hammer in recent years, although Daniels in Brockhurst Road are still flourishing, and appearing to do a very good impersonation of the Murphy tradition of putting plenty on show. Many will remember Fred Daniels who started the business in the 1930's.

In the middle of the last century there was around six ironmongers operating in Gosport, one of the largest of these being the store of Joseph Ponting at No. 115 in the High Street, it was later taken over by Mr. Darby. Darby was certainly a colourful chap, he wore a wide brimmed hat, breeches and gaiters whilst serving in the shop. He carried on helping in the High Street store when it was taken over in the 1870's by John Blake and Son, who traded there for many years into the early part of this century, until the site was taken over by Lipton's in the 1920's.

Being a natural hammer and nail man myself – its very difficult to type with your fingers bandaged – the old style ironmongers were a blessing, for very often they would give sound advice on how to do the job one was trying to tackle. I am pleased to say Stapleton's in Brockhurst Road are still going strong, they have been going for a number of years now, dating back before the last war. In earlier days Vic Hutfield had his garage on the corner of the Harding Road site that Stapleton's now occupy, in fact they still use Vic's old workshop at the rear as a store.

Another old establishment where you could get anything under the sun was at Mr. Park's shop in Stoke Road on the corner of Henry Street, this was popularly known as "Newtown Ironmongery". Strangely enough, the business carried on today from this spot is rather similar, being the premises of Nobes the builders merchants.

Not too far away into the side streets, you would have found George Sherwin's store on the corner of Joseph and Charles Street, and you could get your paraffin from Barnes shop on the other corner. This area is also associated with Grogan's hardware emporium in Charles Street, another veritable wonderland of hardware merchandise.

There was plenty of hardware shops in Forton Road, one of the most popular being Jim Vaux's store a few doors away from the old "Queen Charlotte" pub, he had three sons in the business, Harold looked after the shop and office, Edgar the building department, and Joe took charge of the plumbing side, also we must not forget Charles Albray who managed the shop at one time. Vaux was later taken over by two workers,

Vaux Ironmongery, Forton Road.

who formed Hawkins Brothers the well known Gosport builders.

Vaux's had a fair sized timber yard at the rear of their premises, and the mention of wood reminds us of another timber merchant in Forton Road, for this we will have to go to the beginning of this road, in fact next to the old Parham's site. At No. 4 we would have found Reuben Moody's timber yard in the early part of the century, this spot was later taken over by W. H. Wheeler and Sons whom I mentioned in the first chapter.

William Wheeler started his business in Portsmouth in 1877, his interest at that time was in lath rendering, just one facet of the timber industry. The introduction of the sawn lath led him to trading in timber on a much larger scale, and in 1899 he opened premises in New Road, Portsmouth. His son followed him into the business, followed by his sons, and their sons, a true family concern. The manager at the Gosport branch was Mr. A. Leserve, who was there for many years after having joined the firm in 1924. They still operate from their much expanded Forton Road premises, dealing in timber, builders supplies, and general do-it-yourself.

Still on the subject of wood, I must mention John Goodwillie's timber business in St. Matthews Square, he also had a branch in North Street. I always associate Goodwillie and Co. with our old friend the late Archie Abraham, for he worked there for a number of years during the last war.

After his apprenticeship in the wood trade Archie Abraham started his own furniture factory after the First World War in the Hardway area, he did well and had to expand and move premises many times, just prior to the 1939 hostilities he was well established in the Gosport High Street opposite the Town Hall.

Then came the bombs, Archie was bombed out of the High Street and went to work for Goodwillie's as a temporary measure. After the war he started up on his own again in Forton Road, and many readers will recall starting up home after the war and getting their furniture from the Abraham showroom known as the Towers, next to the Criterion Cinema.

Archie was a true craftsman, his work can be found in many public buildings around the town, including several churches, in fact much of the wood he carried out his skills on came from demolished churches, some of it 400 years old. A leading light in the towns Chamber of Trade and the Rotary Club, and a popular figure as 'Cheerful Charlie' in the old Gosport carnivals, Archie Abraham was sorely missed when he died in 1979 aged 90.

Grogan's Hardware in Charles Street.

Another well known establishment from which many Gosport people have furnished their homes is that of Jeffrey's in Forton Road it was started in 1925 by Reginald Jeffery. The business was originally founded by his father William at Fareham in 1903, from small beginnings in Trinity Street it has developed as a large family furnishing name in both of the two towns.

Still on furniture I must mention Messrs. H. A. Collins who had their premises in Forton Road, and later Stoke Road, they actually made the furniture that they sold. In Stoke Road there was another well established firm of cabinet makers next to the old Union Chapel opposite Stone Lane, their name was Vennelle Brothers, now long gone I am afraid, even Erskine Motors that stood nearby is now history.

Have you noticed how I have veered away from ironmongers? I am very sorry, I am inclined I am afraid to let the typewriter run away from me with my thoughts, Never mind, I hope you enjoyed the digression, now we will get back on course.

A jolly good place to obtain your hardware bits and pieces, especially paints and wallpapers, was Philips in the High Street next to the Congregational Church, or at least next to where it was, the church falling to Hitler's bombs. Hector Philips founded the shop in 1919, catering for builders supplies as well as paint, he also kept a good range of baths, sinks, tools, and even brushes and charcoal sticks for artists and signwriters.

Those days are well remembered by Ernest Jeffery, who as a boy had to make deliveries and collections for Philips on one of those old heavy trades bikes, he recalls that they had a range of 60 wallpapers on show in the window, all at 6d. a roll! The price of paint at that time was 1/9d. for a half-pint tin! The well known Portsmouth firm of Barnes took over from Philips in 1956, Ernest Jeffery became shop manager in 1962 and stayed until his recent retirement, thus completing 51 years of working from the same site. Barnes are still trading there of course, providing our decoration needs.

On the other side of the High Street almost opposite Philips, was aother ironmonger's known as Northcott Stores, although many readers will remember it better from recent years when it was Brighter Homes, another hardware establishment that disappeared in the 1960's.

Another store that just about sold every household item was Hoare & Pilcher in the High Street, on Thorngate Brothers old site, they could not only provide all your needs for lifes living, but even cater for its end with their undertaking service, but more of that later. Originating in Peterborough, Charles Pilcher came to Gosport in 1902 to take over the furnishing

H. J. Philips in the High Street.
Mr. Hector Philips in trilby hat.

business of Mr. J. Hoare, and continued to trade under the title Hoare & Pilcher.

He was a great character in the town, and worked hard for its good, being a member of Gosport U.D.C. he served as Chairman of the Housing Committee immediately prior to the incorporation of Gosport as a Borough, in fact he had the exacting task of organizing the building of the first set of Council houses at Forton. He was the first President of Gosport Rotary Club, served on the Hospital Committee, rode with Hambledon Hounds, Captain of Lee Golf Club, and a Lay Canon of the Diocese of Portsmouth. I wonder what he did in his spare time? He had in fact married Irene the daughter of William Churcher in 1904, and they had three boys

Newtown Ironmongery, Stoke Road.

and three girls, even so he found time to take up the office of Justice of the Peace, so it is certainly true to say that Charles Pilcher was a Gosport trader who left his mark on the town.

I have left space for one more hardware dealer in the true sense of the word, While most folk have heard of a 'Bull in a China Shop', Gosport has in fact a china shop with the name of Bull. Bull's were a very well known name in the Portsmouth area, with many branches stretching out to Chichester. After working in several Portsmouth hardware establishments, Cleveland Duffett joined Bull's in 1923, and soon progressed through the position of manager to that of Director.

Cleveland first came to Gosport in 1932 to manage the branch at Portland buildings in Stoke Road, and has fond

memories of its early days, especially the time he bought 250 galvanized dustbins in a job-lot for 1/10d. each, Bull's gave away a free dustbin to every customer who bought over £1's worth of goods! Mr. Duffett chuckles when he compares the price of dustbins now!

He also recalls when he served as a Special Constable in the last war, one night the Commander came along and exclaimed "Ah, Duffett, just the chap, you can just pop along and clear up your own mess"! Cleveland rushed along to Bull's to find that an incendiary bomb had fallen on the roof and blasted out the windows!

Some of Bull's other branches in Portsmouth and Southsea took a worse hammering, and after the war they faded away from the hardware scene. But the name did not disappear in Gosport, for Cleveland Duffett took over the Stoke Road store in 1953 and I am pleased to say it still flourishes to this day. Cleveland retired in 1970, but left the business to carry on in the capable hands of his son Roger. I am also glad that this store still maintains the old hardware and ironmongers trademark, with plenty of stock outside on the pavement, but not of course china goods, for which Bull's have always been noted.

And that is just about it on this particular subject, although perhaps Timothy Whites might deserve a mention, for although they spread to become a national chain of 140 shops, they did in actual fact start with a small shop in Commercial Road Portsmouth, practically opposite Charlotte Street. Their first Gosport branch was in North Cross Street, then they moved later to the High Street site from which they still operate. One thing is certain, they will never again be able to supply 21-piece tea services for 2/4d.!

Bull's Hardware float in 1930's Gosport Carnival.

CHAPTER NINE

"The Sweet Life"

"Oh I say, Cherry old chap, lend me half-a-crown, I'm expecting a postal order from home tomorrow". This was the favourite plea of Billy Bunter, that famous fat boy from that legendary institution known as Greyfriars, and you could be certain that if our rotund lad did find someone silly enough to lend him money, he would dash straight round to Dame Mimble's Tuckshop to spend it!

If we cast our minds back to days of youth, I expect many of us will have fond memories of our favourite sweetshop from the past, where we would pass over the counter any spare coppers that came our way, and receive in return the sweets of our desire to be shoved into that ever open space underneath our noses. Kids always have, and always will find room for sweets.

With this in mind, I am sure that it has already occurred to you that if you wanted to open a sweetshop, the ideal site would be next to a school, and it is quite amazing how many of the old schools had sweetshops fairly close by. A good example of this was Miss Daisy Henning's sweetshop in Forton road, this was ideally situated as you might say, being sited as it was slam bang next to the old Forton School.

Another spinster lady who shared the name of Daisy, was Miss Daisy Howland who had a confectioners in Bemisters Lane, many readers will have fond memories of this lady, but perhaps not so many will remember her mother who ran the shop before her, Mrs. Eliza Howland. I expect most people who spent their youth in the South Street area will recall the Howland's as will many of the ex-lads from Newtown Boys School remember Kennard's shop in Joseph Street, and pupils

Clifford Munday enjoying the Sweet Life.

from Stone Lane School would have spent their sticky pennies in Mrs. Elliott's sweetshop in Stoke Road, an establishment I am pleased to say is still flourishing under that name.

The proprietors who ran these shops had to have eyes like hawks, while they climbed a shaky pair of steps to get sweets requested from a jar on the top shelf, half of her stock could be cleared by sticky fingers behind her back!

Back in the old days there was a good chance that most of the confectioners got their sweets in Gosport from Munday's Confectionery Supplies in Forton Road, they were wholesalers to the trade for most popular brand names, and they also made some of the sweets themselves. Alfred Munday started his business in 1920 opposite the Forton Barracks and Mill Lane,

before this he had worked for John Parham in the food trade, so Alfred had a good grounding behind him. He also had a small sweet factory out at Peel Common, this was behind the little Evangelical Church, of which Alfred was pastor for 30 years.

The sweets manufactured in the small factory were mostly the boiled variety, and their rock was very popular with young scoffers in the town. Alfred was joined in the 1930's by his son Clifford, and he became a familiar sight driving the Munday van, travelling from sweetshop to sweetshop. And how about some of those pre-war sweet prices, you could have bought a 1lb. casket of Black Magic chocs for three shillings, six Walnut Whips for one shilling, or how about a 3lb. box of Bassetts Liquorice Allsorts for three shillings and sixpence? Nowadays those prices would be more mouth watering than the sweets!

The Munday wholesale confectionery supplies closed down in 1968 after nearly fifty years trading, Alfred the founder died in 1976, but I am pleased to report that Clifford has retained the family connections with the Peel Common church, for his grandparents actually founded the Mission there in 1900.

What's that, eating all those humbugs has made you thirsty, well how about a bottle of pop? There was certainly plenty of this thirst-quenching liquid in the town in the old days, which is not really surprising for we had at least two mineral water companies operating in Gosport. For the first one we must go along to Brockhurst Road and look for Inverness Villa, next to Thistleboon House. This was the site for the Southwell Company, taking its name from the gentleman who owned it, which when you think about it is as good a reason as any.

It was later taken over by Mr. Charles Dwane, and became known as the Brockhurst Mineral Water Company, which I am sure many older readers will remember. The works manager was Herbert Rose, and eventually he took over and owned the business, helped by his wife Emily. Those days are remembered fondly by Gosport resident Cyril Fletcher, who began working for the Rose's in 1921 as a lad of 14, he was a van boy and made deliveries of minerals around the towns shops and pubs.

Trade was seasonal, Winter in the soft drinks trade is like the kiss of death, so Cyril was often out of work in the early days, but I am pleased to say things became more permanent later and he was to stay with the B.M.W. Co. for another twenty years. He went right through the business, from delivering to bottling and blending the syrups. Talking of bottles, do you remember those old glass codd bottles? They were invented by a Mr. Codd, and were rather unique in the fact that they had a glass marble in the neck to control the liquid. But of course, boys being boys they smashed the bottles when empty to get the marbles out! Bet I can roll one closer to the wall than you can!

For our other manufacturer of mineral waters we shall have to travel down to Gosport town itself, I probably have hardly any need to tell you that the establishment we are going to look at has the title "C. Mumby & Co. Ltd. Soda Water Makers to the King and Royal Family".

The business was started by Colonel Charles Mumby in the mid-1800's, who also included in his talents the trade of pharmaceutical chemist, druggist, dentist, ice merchant, and soda water manufacturer. Charles died in 1895 and his son Everitt took over the helm, and he was duly succeeded by his son Charles in the early 1900's.

The most important ingredient for making mineral water is to have pure water, and for this Mumby's were fortunate in having a artesian well within their building in the High Street. The well penetrated through the chalk to a depth of 300ft. below the surface, the water was then pumped to a huge tank

Cyril Fletcher making deliveries for Brockhurst Mineral Water Company at the 'Eagle' in Elmhurst Road.

at the top of the building, from which it passed down through several filters to be refrigerated. Mumby's were also unique in having their own gas making plant, for as well as soda water, various types of minerals and cordials were produced, plus that ever popular beverage, ginger beer.

It was a happy place to work, and when high spirits prevailed syphon fights were quite common amongst the young lads in the works. They had to watch their step though, for most of the staff were females and they had a way of dealing with young lads with cheeky ways, he would find himself quickly de-bagged, and what the ladies did with the syrup that was used in their work, I will leave to your imagination!

Alas, those old mineral water establishments have long since vanished from our town, but occasionally we do get a reminder about them by the discovery of the odd bottle or jar being dug out of the ground, in fact they are now very collectable.

I am afraid we must now say farewell to the 'sweet life', I am sorry I have not mentioned more sweetshops, but through the years they really do add up to a most formidable list. Having said that, I cannot really close without mention of my old friends Jack and Winifred Collins, who will be remembered by many residents for their charming little sweetshop on the corner of Whitworth and Vernon Roads. Winifred really started the shop after the First World War in her maiden name of Peckham, taking it over from Dick Canney the baker. She married jack in 1920, he left his job with the Post Office, and they changed the name on the shops facia to Collins. They ran the sweetshop for 42 years, and now live happily in retirement, a rest well earned.

And so to the next chapter, but before you turn the page, do you think you could lend me half-a-crown until my postal order arrives?

CHAPTER TEN

"Messing About In Boats"

Being sited as it is on the coast, it is obvious that Gosport in one way or another just have connections with the boat-building industry, this has been highlighted by the threatened Dockyard redundancies in recent times, revealing that a good proportion of its workforce cross the harbour to earn their daily crust. Through the years it would be true to say that a great deal of work has been provided also on our Gosport shores for folk who like to earn their living by messing about in boats, so I would like in this chapter to touch briefly upon some of the firms with nautical leanings who have made their presence felt in the town.

The first name that will come into most peoples minds must be that of Camper & Nicholson, renowned boatbuilders throughout the world. For nearly 200 years generations of Gosport families have given devoted service to C. &. N., sons following in their fathers footsteps, and I am pleased to say the tradition has been maintained with this firm still managing to keep their heads above water as it were in this very competitive industry.

It all began in the late 1700's when William Camper started his boatbuilding yard, little could he have known what an empire he was beginning. With hard work and determination he made his chosen business into a successful venture, but it is rather sad that he did not have any suitable relations to pass the firm on to The story goes that one day he had all his young workers assemble in the yard, and from this group he picked out the cleanest and smartest looking lad. The name of this young chap was Benjamin Nicholson, and destiny had decreed that he should be groomed to take the firm over.

Camper & Nicholsons workers in the 1930's.

William Camper's choice proved to be a good one, for Benjamin developed into a very talented boat designer, and when he did eventually take over he began expanding the premises vastly. Dashwood's had a reasonable sized boatyard in Quay Lane, but this did not stop them being swallowed up in the Nicholson plans for expanding.

Benjamin died in 1906 at the age of 78, and his son Charles took over the helm, he had inherited his fathers design skills and know-how, and it was under his guidance that during the following thirty years the Gosport yard enjoyed its most successful times.

Although C. & N. built a great variety of craft, it was always the racing yachts that hit the headlines and provided the glamour, beautiful sleek creatures such as the Nyria and the Brynhild slid gracefully into the sea from the Gosport shore. But it was in 1913 that the interest of the world looked towards Gosport, Sir Thomas Lipton the millionaire grocer had his eye on capturing the America's Cup, with this in mind he commissioned Charles Nicholson to build his famous Shamrock IV racing yacht.

These were marvellous days for the town, highlighted when Lipton came personally to see progress. They were casting the lead keel that day, and being the born showman that he was he dipped into his waistcoat pockets and threw a handful of gold sovereigns into the casting. You can imagine how the watching workers felt about that action, a sovereign would have fed their families for a week!

As history has shown Shamrock IV failed in her cup attempt after the 1914-18 war, but C. & N. kept churning splendid yachts off the assembly line, amongst them the Astra in 1928, the Candida in 1929, followed by the Shamrock V in 1930. Then Tommy Sopwith the aircraft millionaire entered the yachting scene and came to Gosport in 1934 to launch The

Camper & Nicholson's.

Endeavour, and returned a couple of years later for Endeavour II, but sadly all attempts failed and the Americans kept the cup. But even in failure, these magnificent sailing vessels from the Camper and Nicholson boatyard provided a wonderful boost for Gosport generally, and they are days that we will probably never see again. Having said that, a reminder of those days of glory was re-enacted recently when Gosport provided the base for the start of the Whitbread Around-the-World race, the town was invaded by great yachts and crews from all over the globe to provide a festive atmosphere that was akin to days gone by.

Of course those yachts would not have been of much use if they had not got sails, and that was indeed another product

Ratsey & Lapthorn's sail loft.

that was manufactured in Gosport, and therefore another industry that provided work for the townsfolk. Around the middle of the last century we had three chief sailmaking establishments in the town, there were the lofts of Richard Avery at North Beach, those of Cunnningham on The Green, and the third will be a name that most people will recall more readily, that of Ratsey and Lapthorn.

The firm was founded by James Lapthorn in 1825, he came across from Devon to perform this task and was later joined by his sons to make the business a great success. They were really on to a good thing, for in those days sail ruled supreme. James died in 1869, and so did his eldest son, so another son named Edwin was left to carry on the family tradition at the age of 36.

Edwin had his eye on Miss Matilda Field who was the daughter of a well known Gosport solicitor named Thomas Field, anyway Matilda became Mrs. Lapthorn and in the following years she presented him with three sons and six daughters!

There were big changes at Lapthorns in 1882, they amalgamated with another sail firm from Cowes in the Isle of Wight named Ratsey. George Ratsey had one son and five daughters, so he and Edwin had a lot in common away from the lofts, but in the lofts they also proved to be a dynamic duo and the partnership produced a great deal of expansion. Ratsey and Lapthorn became known world-wide, and their sails were much sought after by yacht owners in particular after sail gave way to steam on larger vessels.

Edwin Lapthorn did a great deal of work on behalf of Gosport, acting as Chairman on several local companies such as gas and water, and also gave good service as a local Magistrate. His death was a sad loss to the town in 1918, a great team came to an end, and George Ratsey the other half died himself in 1922.

The business carried on, despite the main loft being destroyed by enemy bombs during the last war, it was replaced in 1949 by a two-storey building in Clarence Square. It was in this building that they could boast of having the largest sail loft in the world, 150ft. by 45ft. This was filled almost completely by the largest cross-cut spinnaker made since the war, it was for the "Creole" luxury yacht of Greek millionaire Stavros Niarchos, in all 8,500 sq. ft. of sail!

But the name of Ratsey and Lapthorn eventually disappeared from the Gosport scene, they moved their operations to Cowes where they still dominate the waterline, and so the town lost yet another of its famous institutions.

Still dealing with boats and accessories, the name Algecide Anti-Fouling Company may cause a few heads to be scratched, they were incorporated in 1898 and had various premises around the town including Mount Street and the High Street, but in 1937 they moved to Harbour Road and are now more popularly known as Blakes Paints.

While in Harbour Road we must mention our old friend George Watts who built yachts for many years in his premises there, or Reg Rogers who not only made them but also gave boat rides for anyone who fancied a trip on the briny for the princely sum of 6d., usually from Stokes Bay.

Well landlubbers, you can stop swallowing your seasick pills now, we are returning to dry land and a look at a few more Gosport traders.

CHAPTER ELEVEN
"My Feet Ache, It Must Be Getting Near Closing Time"

For any reader who has ever worked in a shop, they will know exactly what I mean when I refer to the 'magic hour', it is that particular time towards the end of the working day when the hands of the clock move nearer to the moment when the guv'nor ejects those magic words "Right, that's it, lock the front door, its time we went home".

We needed no second telling, it was a case of overcoat on, onto our push-bikes, and a fast ride home to tell Mum what a terrible day we had gone through, and how our feet ached terribly!

Well, it is getting close to that 'magic hour' when space tells me that the time is rapidly approaching for me to pull down the shutters on this book, so in this last but one chapter I shall be throwing in as many traders names and establishments as I possibly can in a valiant attempt to please as many folk as possible. But be warned, it will be rather like one of those T.V. quiz games where contestants have to name as many tunes as they can in three minutes!

And that's as good a start as I could wish for, I mentioned the word tune, this gets me to thinking immediately about Wood's Violin Shop in Bemisters Lane, I expect many budding musicians went to get their music sheets there, for William Wood was the towns main musical instrument dealer for many years. William had a son who was very musical, in fact he played a cello in that popular gosport dance band of pre-war days that performed under the baton of Harry Barnard. Do you remember them? Good old days!

A few lines ago I mentioned the word push-bike, this conjures up for me a recollection of my youth when I turned out at six o'clock every morning to do a paper round that eventually allowed me to buy my first bicycle, I remember that old bike well, it had only had 64 previous owners! Off I would go every Sunday to discover pastures new and enjoy the delights of the open road, nowadays you would be lucky to get as far as Wickham without being grazed by the paint of passing cars!

Can you remember where you bought your first bike, there was certainly plenty of bike dealers to choose from, and fortunately some of those old names are still with us. Take Turner's for instance in Stoke Road, Ralph Turner founded his business there over 50 years ago, and I am pleased to say the name has been retained. Some readers may be surprised to learn that it was a cycle shop when Mr. Turner took it over, it was in fact run by a gent named William Pearce.

Another well known name in Gosport's cycle dealer world is that of Spragg's in Forton Road, the business was started by Samuel Spragg when he was demobbed from the Royal Artillery, the regiment not the pub, in 1920. Those were the days when bicycles ruled the road, the horseless carriage had not really taken over as yet. Anyway, the business has passed through the family down to a third generation Spragg, namely Maurice.

Older readers may remember another cycle dealer not far from the Spragg site in Forton Road, the proprietor revelled in the marvellous name of Hezekiah Mason, and if my memory serves me correctly he also ran a private bus around the Hardway area.

I think I have space for one more bicycle agent, how about Clarence Cory down in the High Street, you may recall he and his father had premises near the old Electricity offices. This site was later taken over by Woolworth's 3d. & 6d. Stores,

Turner's Cycle Shop, Stoke Road.

those were the days, so Clarence moved across to the other side of the High Street. His father William Cory came over from Jersey in 1871 to start a coachbuilding business, which son Clarence took over in 1914, then William died ten years later in 1924 at the age of 84.

There was another Gosport family who had dealings in the motor trade in later years, but started off by selling and repairing bicycles in their early days, this was the North Street establishment of Edward Lee on the corner of Sea Horse Street. Ed was a very clever chap, in 1914 he invented and had patented a special lock for bicycles. He was also one of the founders of the Gosport Conservative Club and at one time served as Chairman, when he died in 1925 aged 60, Sir John Davidson the M.P. paid a special tribute.

While in the North Street area I simply must mention French's the pharmacists, sorry, there I go again, getting all posh, I should have said chemists. Ben French started as a dispenser at Haslar Hospital, but later opened his own business in North Street, and even later moved to North Street just past the Crown Hotel. Ben was also a very popular Baptist Minister at Brockhurst, up until his death at the age of 89 in 1916. Readers may be more familiar with the French premises when it was later taken over by Wilson's the chemists, and even later when it was Jenkins.

Chemists were great ones for banging the sales drum in the old days, and were always proclaiming miracle cures for every ailment under the sun. French's claimed the wonders of their special Infants and Invalids Food, a bargain at 8d. for a pound tin. While Charles Upson from his establishment in Stoke Road seemed to be most concerned about mosquito and gnat bites, and a bottle of his very special lotion could be purchased in 6d. or 1/- bottles. On the other hand, Charlie Kent's chemist shop in Forton Road on the corner of Alexandra Street was worried about animal ailments, and of course had available a variety of pills and powders, but it was noticeable that for humans he strongly recommended the wonders of Wincarnis.

Now for false teeth the place to go was Mr. Smith the chemist in the High Street, he advertised upper or lower sets from 30/-, or a single tooth at only 3/-. Smith's also had a shop in Forton Road, although the premises in the High Street will feature most prominently in readers minds, especially during the war when it fell a victim to enemy bombs. Greenburghs the Tailors now occupy that particular site. I must close the subject of Gosport chemists now, but I expect lots of people will remember Chase the Chemist in Anns Hill Road, and of course Darling's in Stoke Road where we used to take films from our Brownie Box Camera's to be developed and printed.

Fletcher's and Hales shops in Forton Road, corner of Leonard Road.

It was quite on the cards that you may have wanted those photographs mounted in a picture frame, and of course the place to go was our old friend Mr. Collins in Forton Road. The son of a Forton marine, Martin Henry Collins was given his christian names after that of the famous rifle, and this led in later life to him being referred to as "A Son of a Gun".

Through a school injury Martin was unable to realize his ambition and join the Marines, so he started his frame business in 1894 at the age of 19, it proved to be a great success, and in fact the famous Snape family of artists were regular customers. Martin Collins also opened a shop a little further down Forton Road where he dealt for a while in bicycles, but later turned it into a bazaar with his sister Sarah in charge, it was a kind of forerunner to Woolworth's with most items ranging from 1d to 6d.

Martin was married to Bertha, who presented him with two sons and one daughter, the boys Henry and Martin turned their hands to furniture making and built-up the successful business that I mentioned in a previous chapter, but his daughter Dorothy has carried on the family framing shop in Forton Road. Dorothy remembers the old days well, when her Dad would go out to deliver the framed pictures after the shop had closed for the day, the kids would always walk with him there, but were sure to get a ride home in the little trolley cart he made deliveries in. Martin Collins always had one pint of beer a day in the "Five Alls" on the corner, and it could not have done him much harm for he died in 1948 at the age of 73. I expect many readers will recall another picture frame maker in North Cross Street, this was the premises of John Turner, he later moved to the High Street near the old Town Hall.

Do you remember when Mum used to drag us lads down to the barbers shop for what was commonly referred to as a 'short, back and sides', when we would walk around for weeks after looking like 'Convict 99'. Some of the girls were just as bad, sporting what may be called "pudding-basin" cuts! Of course folk are a lot more fussy about their hair nowadays, and even I have got over my horror of visiting the barbers by paying my monthly visit to hairdressers such as Ian Antony in Brockhurst Road, where pudding-basins and sheep shears have been abolished in favour of cutting and styling. The only snag is that I have less hair to attend to now!

Well, lets get down to naming just a few hairdressers from the past, it is interesting to note that in the late 1700's there was a number of hairdressers in Gosport, and that the men wore their hair in a high peak like the ladies, they also wore pigtails. The ladies had a bit of a performance with their coiffeur, they did their hair on a wire frame 18" high and combed up from the forehead.

In the 1850's there was a hairdressers in the High Street near the King's Arms run by Jim Cobbett, then this was taken over in later years by John Douglass who was in business there for many years until his death in 1907. Some readers may remember Jim Pullen who also worked from this shop with his skilled scissors, but by the 1930's it was the site for Fred Dade's fish shop.

Russell's in Stoke Road was also very popular for a bit off the top, and it may not be remembered that he was also an umbrella maker, and his great offer was to re-cover umbrellas for 2/11d., but I hope he did not do it while cutting hair! Although the name of Oliver Russell had disappeared from the facia, it has remained a hairdressing salon for many years under the well known proprietorship of Hunt's.

The list could go on and on, but here are a few more to jog the memory, Fred Callard in North Cross Street, John Allen in Bemisters Lane, Conway in Forton Road, also John Couper in Forton Road, and Bill Gouge who ran his barbers shop for many years in San Diego, this is the establishment that was later taken over by our old friend Jack Blake, who in his youth worked at the old Olympia Cinema in Stoke Road.

We must quickly mention the ladies, and I am sure the name Maison Charles will come readily to the minds of most hair conscious ladies, and so will the name Roland Hill. In fact back in 1937 there was a rather interesting court case in Gosport in which Violet Collins the owner of a tobacconists shop in the High Street, sued Roland Hill's High Street salon for damages while undergoing a one guinea perm to her hair. She claimed the shop was negligent because the curling process was too tight, with too much heat and too much ammonia, plus the fact she was left under the dryer too long, resulting in head pains and her hair dropping out in bald patches. But she lost the case with the court eventually deciding that a nervous disorder had caused her hair to fall out!

Before leaving hairdressers and the High Street I will mention Charlie Standhaft's salon in that throughfare, it was a favourite place for the bus and tram crews to visit for a haircut, they gave a hoot as they went past so that he would have a chair ready and waiting for them, much to the disgust of his other customers!

Mentioning the word tobacconist a few lines ago could easily send us up another avenue, there was certainly plenty of them, then this would lead on to newsagents, for many of us bought our packet of Woodbines in such establishments. So for the sake of space I will drift fairly lightly over this subject, but next to Standhaft's was a very old established newsagents in the shape of Holmes. Allen Holmes opened a shop in North Street in 1880, later in Bemisters Lane, and then in 1888 he moved to the High Street shop that he was to run for 40 years, until his death in 1928. A kind man, and much respected member of the Wesleyan Church, he left five sons. Another well known name in the town that I am pleased to state is still flourishing in Stoke Road is the establishment of Herbert Bartlett, selling fags and papers now for well over 60 years.

Before leaving tobacco, I know that many readers who smoke will have fond memories of getting their smokes from Sammy Hall's kiosk and later expanded to provide a film developing and printing service. In 1939 he opened another branch in St. Matthews Sq., and another in Stoke Road in the following year. Sammy now lives happily in retirement, and still does a lot of charity work by collecting money for the N.S.P.C.C.

Of course some folk like their reading to be a little more fulfilling than newspapers, and the strange thing is that Gosport had far more bookshops back in the last century than we have had in this, I suppose the discovery of films, radio and television have contributed towards this state of affairs. Our oldest established bookshop in the town is that of the Gosport Bookshop, but more popularly remembered as Miles. Mr. Miles opened the shop in 1938, and although many lines such as sweets and tobacco have been discontinued, I am pleased to say that the business under his son Pat Miles is very alive with the sale of books, staionery and art materials, and in fact supplied the typing paper that I am pounding on this very moment. So its the Gosport Bookshop for new books, but how about old books? This aspect has been a literary desert in Gosport for some time, so I am pleased to see that Richard Martin has opened a shop in Stoke Road for old books and prints. I personally hope for the day when folk will come back to more reading and less television viewing! Its a lot quieter!

Of course, books have to be printed, and Gosport has quite a long history in this field, in fact it was the first place to set up a printing press in the area, this was done by a Mr. Philpot whose first job was printing the churchwardens accounts for the Alverstoke Parish in 1798. In more recent years the firm of Gosport Printing has given a good printing service for the town, and the name of Harry Cooley a former Gosport Mayor will be associated with its foundation.

But the title of the longest running establishment in the town for printing must go to Kemp Brothers & Wooton, who have celebrated 75 years of printing in the town. The founder was a Dr. John Wallace Kemp, after serving in the Boer War he came to Gosport to open a stationers shop in the High Street. He received so many orders for printing he established a small works, this was so successful he formed a company with his brother Walter and a salesman named Wooton.

About 1910 John decided to return to his first love of medicine, and sold his shares to Mr. Dotterill and Mr. Johnson who ran the printing side of the works. Dotterill died in 1926, and Mr. Johnson's son-in-law later became a Director. Mr. R. D. Rogers joined the company in 1928 as a Director, he was a son of Sanders Rogers whom I mentioned in the chapter on bakers.

Originally the firm operated from Ashby Works off the High Street, but this was destroyed by enemy bombs in World War Two. It was not long before they were back in business on a new site, this was in White Hart Road near the old Gosport Road Station. Dennis Rogers died in the late 1970's, but the firm has been carried on by his son-in-law Gordon Lenn, and is still thriving from the same White Hart site. I might add that K. B. & W. have created something of a record through the years for the loyalty of their workers, many of whom completed over 50 years service to the firm.

I mentioned Sidney Smith the North Cross Street pawnbroker in an earlier chapter but of course he was chiefly noted as a jeweller, in 1914 he could provide good tough gents watches for 5/6d., engraved silver watches from 5/9d., and gold watches from 18/6d.! Sidney served on the Board of Guardians at one time, and was a popular member of the Queens Bowling Club, he died at the age of 73 in 1924.

George Dukes was another renowned Gosport jeweller who put in a good deal of hard work for the good of the town, and will be remembered for his shop next to the Gosport Theatre by older residents, they may even have bought his special line of rolled gold spectacles there for five bob a pair, sight tested of course. George first came to Gosport from Aylesbury in 1881 to work for Mr. Stubbington the Stoke Road jeweller, he took the business over in 1883 and a number of years later moved to his High Street premises. He was elected to the council in 1902, and was a leading force in the campaign for the town to become a borough, in fact he was strongly fancied for the post of First Mayor. But fate played its hand, George Dukes died from a car accident in the High Street in 1920.

I have just mentioned Henry Stubbington, in his earlier years he had a jewellers in the High Street at No. 46, and next to him at No. 44 was George King the clockmaker. In fact in the 1860's there was several watchmakers and jewellers in that particular section of the High Street. I expect there are still a few examples of their craftsmanship still around, in fact quite recently an excellent wall clock made by King came to my notice with the letters 'VR' on the face.

From the time when prehistoric man placed a stick in the ground and told his old woman to wake him up when the shadow fell across his face, man has been increasingly time-conscious. Little did he know that in years to come folks would be able to buy a magic time-stick from establishments such as Hug's to wear on their wrists. We always associate Switzerland with time-pieces, and this is in fact where the old established jewellery family of Gosport had their origins. The present families grandfather came to the town complete with watchmakers tools and yodel in the 1890's, this was in the North Cross Street area, then his son William James Hug took over from him and opened a shop in the High Street at No. 82, there was also a branch at Ventnor on the Isle of Wight. William's three sons carried on the trade, the eldest is another William and he runs his business in Stoke Road, whilst his two brothers Dennis and Richard run the High Street establishment.

The other well known name in this trade as far as Gosport is concerned is that of Ruff, they are of course still flourishing in the High Street. Mark Henry Ruff opened a jewellers shop in Stoke Road in 1906, he later moved to London leaving his son

Cyril to carry on, and he moved to larger premises in 1926 at 7a, Stoke Road, then in 1959 they moved to their present site in the High Street. Cyril had more or less retired in 1948, leaving his son Ken to take-over, helped by his wife Eileen. I am pleased to report that their sons Ian and Kevin are also in the business, thus carrying on the family name and tradition.

I must now pull the shutters down on jewellers. Whats that? I have not mentioned Bolitho's in the High Street! Oh, alright then, Francis Bolitho was another well known jeweller who had his shop on the corner of South Cross Street, where Fiarhall & Durston now have their estate agency. So there!

But I shall certainly not delve into the world of estage agents now, there was certainly plenty of them, Paine & Marsh, Llewellyn Puttock, L. S. Vail, and many more through the years. Instead, I shall quickly flick onto the bricks and mortar that they deal in, or to be more precise the builders that erect the property.

The building trade has provided plenty of work for local tradesmen for many years, in fact on many of the contracts for building projects in the past it was clearly stipulated that a specified percentage of local workforce should be used. Son followed father very often in the trade, and more often than not they both worked for the same builder. The mammoth building concern of John Hunt's has a fine record for this tradition, so let us begin with them.

John Hunt came to Gosport in the late 1800's as a general manager for J. & M. Patrick a Rochester builder, engaged in building the Zymotic Hospital at Haslar and various large buildings at Priddys Hard. John went into business for himself in 1902 and one of his first contracts was for the erection of the Superintendents house in Gosport Park, but his first large contract was for the Fire Station in Clarence Road.

A branch was opened at Winchester in 1910, and this

Gosport Brick Works,
off Bury Hall Lane area c. 1907.

continued until the end of the First World War, but Gosport was the main base for operations. Although he concentrated on government and public works, John Hunt also developed part of Peel Road, Village Road, and the Portland Buildings in Stoke Road. In the inter-war years he built council houses at Portchester, Fareham, Titchfield and Stubbington, as well as contracts to develop Grange and Lee-on-the-Solent aerodromes.

After the war the emphasis was on housing, but in the following years they played a big part in the large shop and office development in Portsmouths' Commercial Road. The company by this time was run by the founders grandsons John and Pat Hunt, it has remained a family concern. The name of

John Hunt has proudly been displayed to the fore of many large projects in recent years, and can currently be seen on the new extensions for Gosport's War Memorial Hospital, a building that they erected originally in 1923.

Another building firm of note in our area is that of Croad's, they were founded way back in 1830 in Portsmouth by Johnothan Croad. His son John started up in Gosport in 1885 at their High Street premises, and in 1916 he opened up in Fareham, and even the Isolation Hospital at Elson. John Croad was a great character in the town, and could be seen regularly in the cycling around Gosport on his old bicycle. One of my favourite Croad structures in the town was the old Gas Showrooms they built in the High Street in 1913, however did a piece of architecture like that get demolished?

I must briefly mention the Hawkins building empire that was begun by Fareham brothers Richard and Stanley Hawkins in 1936, starting as builders, decorators and ironmongers. They started building houses in 1938, and their first contract after the war was 50 houses for G.B.C. By 1959 they employed 430 people and had built over 2,500 houses, plus schools, churches, factories, the Bury Cross Fire Station, the Police Station and Magistrates Court, Northcott House, Bay House Grammar Schol, and much more!

Just two more names, we cannot leave out the building firm of Rose who have maintained a family tradition in Gosport for their work, or Bailey and Stride who entered the scene in 1949 and took over a former laundry in Whitworth Road for premises and workshops. The name of that laundry? Flux's of course.

So much for the builders, how about the houses? Well, eat your heart out when I tell you that you could have bought a small family house in 1925 for £275, or if you were really flush a 4-bedroomed house in Anglesey Road for £1,000, and if you were in the tycoon class you could have had a 6-bedroomed mansion in Monckton Road for £1,600!

And so, as the sun has set on revered corn merchants such as the Millard Brothers in Clarence Road, and Dittman and Malpas in the High Street, so it must set on this chapter. Let's face it, if I do not close the chapter soon it will be longer than "Gone With The Wind", and this book will cost twenty quid a copy!

Now for the final chapter, and when you look at the subject I am sure you will agree that you cannot get more final than this! Not in this life anyway!

CHAPTER TWELVE

"When You've Gotta Go, You Gotta Go"!

The Gosport to Portsmouth Floating Bridge ground onto the beach at Point in Old Portsmouth, and the horse-drawn vehicles that it had carried across began to slowly make the steep ascent from vessel to roadway. Most goods were transported via this sea crossing in the old days, from coal carts to cattle, from brewers drays to funeral hearses.

In fact it was a funeral cart that was climbing the ferry slope at that moment, a Gosport undertaker was transporting a body to Southsea. As the horses struggled up the steep rise the cart began to vibrate alarmingly, with the result that the coffin it was carrying fell off the back!

Onlookers watched in horror as the wooden box slid back down the slope and into the water, then gradually drift out into the harbour before anyone could get hold of it! Our undertaker friend had the embarassing experience of having to hire a boat and row out to tow it in!

Of course this happened many years ago, unless the deceased is Royalty the practice of pulling a hearse by horses has disappeared, and so unfortunately has the dear old Floating Bridge. Customs also seem to have gone by the board, and respect with it, do you remember when the sight of a funeral procession would immediately prompt pedestrians to stop on the pavement and take off their hats to clutch to their chests, and servicemen would stop and salute if the deceased was an old soldier or sailor. Things are a lot different now, I have seen impatient motorists honk hearses while attempting to overtake them.

Undertaking is one trade that will never be hit by lack of customers, hence my title when the Good Lord calls, then that is it. But the funeral business canfluctuate according to season, this was borought home to me by my old Uncle Bill, an ex-policeman who in his retirement earnt a bit extra filling in as a coffin bearer. Being very tall as he was, and the only one in the family who owned a black overcoat, Uncle Bill was what you would term a natural for the job! I can remember him now, looking out the window at the grey skies and saying: "There's a cold east wind out there, we are going to be busy next week". Of course in the end those cold east winds caught up with Uncle Bill, and he had his last ride on someone elses shoulders.

Funerals were certainly more pretentious affairs in earlier times, some folk appear to harbour the notion that it was not what you did in this world that counted, it was the way you left it that mattered. Hence the common sight of glass-sided hearses drawn by dark horses with black plumes on their foreheads, very often with attendants walking by the side of the coaches.

One of the most spectacular funerals to be seen in Gosport undoubtedly happened in the early half of the last century, this was when a Queen of Spain, Donna Franscisca, died whilst staying at Alverstoke Rectory. Her body lay in state for several days at the Rectory beneath a canopy of crimson cloth, eighteen candles were kept burning for her servants to pay homage.

The arrangements were put in the hands of Mr. Cook the Gosport undertaker, the hearse was drawn by eight horses with six pages walking at the side, there were also six mutes on horseback in cloaks and mourning hats. As if this was not spectacle enough, the band of the Royal Marines were also on show playing the Funeral March of George the Fourth, and it was estimated that 60,000 people lined the route from Anglesey to the Roman Catholic Church in Gosport. The Royal personage was interred there, and later her remains taken to Spain.

Cartwright's in Stoke Road, c. 1912.

Mr. Crook no doubt did very well from that affair, and was the envy of his profession in our town, but lets face, this job is not everyones cup of tea, and calls for a very special kind of person. I am pleased to report that we have had quite a number of these special people through the years supplying their service in the town, I cannot possibly name them all in this chapter, but will never the less attempt to touch upon a few more familiar names from this century.

Many undertakers appeared to take it on as a sideline to supplement their main trade, such as builders, house furnishers or even the drapery trade. Concerning the latter business the name of Cartwright in Stoke Road comes immediately to mind, they could either stretch your elastic, or stretch you out! Ben Cartwright was a tall dignified gent who looked immediately at ease in a long black frock-coat and topper, he had two daughters who served in the store selling materials, ribbons, elastic, buttons, and so on. Cartwright's premises were more or less on the site that is occupied by the more recently built Oasis Restaurant and card shop.

Farther along Stoke Road was the well known business of Churcher's associated with funeral arrangements, but they were also prominent as specialists in monumental and ornamental masonry. Started by William Henry Churcher in 1867, the business comprised a spacious showroom in Stoke Road, with his stoneyard at the rear. Just getting the stone from Gosport Railway Station must have been like the building of Stonehenge, some of the blocks weighed twelve tons, and liable to make most carts and their horses creak with the strain for sure. The struggle was not really over when the stone was unloaded in the yard, a sawyer would then have to cut the stone in half by handsaw, a task which sometimes took a week!

As well as supplying those beautiful gravestones, absolute works of art, Churcher's also made most of the stone bay

William Churcher's Monumental Works in Stoke Road.

windows for houses in Queens, Kings, Percy, Blake, and Elmhurst Roads. Study the workmanship if you have the opportunity, and imagine how it was carried out with tools that would now be looked upon as ancient. In later years the business was concentrated more on the funeral side, but it remained a family firm I am pleased to say, with William passing it on to his son Percy, and in turn it was taken over by his son Nigel Churcher.

Churcher's only rivals as such in the monumental masonry trade was Charles Chase's establishment in Anns Hill Road, nice and handy for Anns Hill Cemetery nearby. This site is now occupied, the stonemasons not the cemetery, by the Gosport Printing Works on the corner of Westfield Road.

Osborn's, North Cross Street.

But for a brief moment let us return to Stoke Road, older readers may recall that there was an undertaker near the beginning of this road at No. 3, the funeral director there was Stephen Hopkins, he also had premises on the other side of the road on the corner of Prince of Wales Road at one time. Although the site by No. 3 has changed hands and varying businesses since the war years, it is interesting to note that in recent times it has reverted to the funeral trade through the name of Tribbeck & Churcher.

Let us continue down to the High Street, I have already mentioned that Hoare and Pilcher acted as funeral directors as well as house furnishers, but if we stroll not so many yards away into North Cross Street we would have found another name that combined house furnishing and undertaking, the premises of H. D. Osborn.

Henry Osborn originally ran a funeral parlour in Ryde on the Isle of Wight, then he moved his family over the water in 1893 to take over the business of his father-in-law, Mr. Merrington. Henry built up a good trade, with funeral service, furnishing, china and glassware. He also worked hard for the town and served on the Urban District Council and the Borough Council, he was a churchman at St. Matthews, a prominent freemason, and started the first chess club in Gosport.

Henry Osborn died in 1928 at the age of 64, and the North Cross Street business was carried on by his two sons Jehu and Charles. Of course, Charles will be remembered for his work on the council also, and for the fact that he served as the Mayor of Gosport in 1949 for four years.

Charles wife Rose was also involved in the business, this came in the form of flowers and wreaths, and strangely enough the wife of our next undertaking name also carried out this side of the trade. But let us go back to the beginning, in North

Hoare & Pilcher, 1926 Advert.

Street there was a cabinet maker named William Crossland, he was referred to as Junior because his father whose name was also William was a furniture dealer in Forton Road. Well, William Junior also branched out in the funeral business helped by his son Eddie. The lad worked from 7.30 in the morning till 6.30 at night, all for the princely sum of one shilling a week. If the deceased died away from home he would be returned to his house by the undertaker in the hours of darkness, this meant that the undertaker could work a 70 to 80 hour week!

But Eddie learnt his trade well and took over when his father William died in 1930 at the age of 55, his mother died at the age of 90, and Eddie recalls that she weighed 27-stone. But

*Stoke Road view c. 1910.   Including Barratt's the butchers and
Russell's Hairdressing Salon.*

*Pimco Ice-Cream seller in Woodley Road,
Gosport 1935.*

even this pales when compared with the coffin he had to
provide for a lady weighting 40-stone, it took ten men to lift it
off the ground! Eddie Crossland is one of the few undertakers
in the area who is also qualified as an embalmer.

The Crossland business moved to the site they still occupy in
Forton Road, and where his wife Nora also featured with her
flowers and wreath skills until her death in recent months.
Eddie Crossland has also played a big part in the towns
sporting life, in football, golf, and in swimming. He still does
in fact maintain an interest in the St. Vincent Swimming Club.

The above does highlight the need for people in the undertaking profession to have outside interests, I know that Nigel
Churcher did a good deal of charity work for the Mansfield
Blind Home in Lee-on-the-Solent in his spare time. They have
to, for if you thought about your work in this particular line it
would get very depressing. As I have stated previously,
undertakers are a very special breed of chaps.

CHAPTER THIRTEEN

"Pulling Down The Shutters"

That's it, the day is over and those poor old shop assistants can now trundle off home and put their feet up. But first, I must turn the sign on the door around to 'CLOSED'.

This is the moment when I don my hat and dark glasses, and put on my false beard before venturing into the outside world. I am sure that some little old lady or gentleman will approach me and whack me with their umbrella because I did not mention their Auntie Nellie who had a sweetshop in Gosport!

I am sorry, it was like trying to get a quart into a pint pot! Before putting finger to typewriter I vowed to myself that I would aim at mentioning at least 200 traders names from the past, as this figure actually went over 250 I feel that I have provided reasonable value.

I have no doubt that many readers will have memories of several other traders and professions, such as coal merchants, wallpaper manufacturers, nurserymen, restaurants, and many more. Regarding the latter, I promise that I shall bring the Tomlinson family of 'Dive' fame into a future book about transport. Two other deliverate omissions are public houses and photographers, these are such vast subjects they will also be featured seperately in books of this series to be found in your bookshop in the very near future.

Until then, I hope you have enjoyed this nostalgic and factual look-back on some of Gosport's traders and businesses from the past. Personally, I would like to think of it as my small tribute to those who have served behind a counter and have patiently dealt with the trials and tribulations that customers can sometimes bring. Yes, people the calibre of Sid Ashby who has worked in Gosport High Street for Milletts Menswear shop for over fifty years. This book is for them, the dedicated folk with the perpetual smile on their faces who stepped forward to say: "Good Morning, Are You Being Served"?

Is this you –
or your Estate Agent?

Saving the £500-£1000 your estate agent would charge to sell an average house or flat could buy you a superb holiday for two. Instead of paying for your estate agent's holiday, you could sell your property through Homeline — at a cost of around £60.

With Homeline, you can sell privately and discreetly, highlighting the features that mean most to you. There are no hidden extras, and **no commission on sale.**

For buyers the service is free — you give us your requirements, and we'll send you details of properties that match, putting you in touch with the seller direct.

Our Hayling Island office covers the Solent area from Bognor Regis to Southampton and extends to Winchester and Midhurst. What estate agent can so effectively give such wide coverage from a single office?

The Homeline service helps you with surveys, mortgages and conveyancing — in fact everything you need when you move. We have offices throughout the Midlands, the West, the South and the London area. For more information **Phone Hayling Island 67142**

Regal House, Mengham Road, Hayling Island, Hants. **Homeline**

The real alternative to estate agents. And their fees.

High Street decorated for Coronation of George V.

1.

High Street, Gosport

2.

3.

4.

5.

6.

The Victory Restaurant, Gosport.

HOT DINNERS from the Joint. THREE VEGETABLES.

PRICES TO SUIT ALL CLASSES. **6d., 9d., 1/- & 2/-**

HAM, BEEF, PORK. **TEAS.**

7.

Captions:
1. High Street.
2. High Street.
3. North Street.
4. Northcross Street. Street Football Broadcast.
5. Clarence Road in Tramway Days.
6. Co-op Bakery, Elmhurst Road.
7. How about a Dinner for 6d. 1905 prices.